ART EDUCATION
during
ADOLESCENCE

BOOKS ON ART EDUCATION AVAILABLE FROM THE
ONTARIO DEPARTMENT OF EDUCATION

Art Education in the Kindergarten
Art Education for Slow Learners
Art Education during Adolescence
Art and Crafts in the Schools of Ontario
Children and Their Pictures

ART EDUCATION
during
ADOLESCENCE

ONTARIO
PREPARED BY THE CURRICULUM DIVISION
Ontario Department of Education

THE RYERSON PRESS — TORONTO

COPYRIGHT, CANADA, 1954, BY
THE RYERSON PRESS, TORONTO

All rights reserved. No part of this book may be reproduced in any form (except by reviewers for the public press), without permission in writing from the publishers.

Fourth Printing, 1970

PRINTED AND BOUND IN CANADA
BY THE RYERSON PRESS, TORONTO

INTRODUCTION

THIS BOOK APPEARS AFTER NEARLY SIX YEARS OF RESEARCH WITH adolescents engaged in art activities. When the Ontario Department of Education, in 1948, inaugurated a programme of research in art, the first project undertaken was an investigation into the nature of an art programme suitable for young people enrolled in the seventh to the twelfth grades of schools within the provincial system of education. Although other research projects during the six years received attention, only this one on the subject of adolescence has remained to be concluded.

Several reasons have caused the research to span so many years. Perhaps the chief of these lies in the fact that adolescence is a period of great physical, intellectual, emotional and social change. It was found necessary, therefore, to study some individuals during the entire time in which they were passing through the several stages of adolescence in order to observe and to compare the characteristics of one stage with another. Two hundred pupils were studied in this manner. In order to discover solutions to other problems, larger numbers of adolescents were studied but for shorter periods. Altogether, pupils in 240 schools in the Province assisted in one way or another in compiling this report.

This volume deals with topics ranging from a consideration of the physical, intellectual, emotional and social patterns of development found during each period of adolescence, to discussion of classroom accommodation, teaching methods and art activities related to the needs of young people developing from the end of childhood to the beginning of adulthood. Wherever possible and practical the statements made herein about these topics have been carefully analyzed and tested in classroom situations.

INTRODUCTION

The assistance of numerous people in completing this book must be acknowledged with many thanks. Among them are included officials in the Ontario Department of Education in both the Elementary and the Secondary School Branches who read the manuscript and offered suggestions for its improvement, the Technical Advisers in the Department who provided data concerning plans for art rooms, the departmental Director of the Audio-Visual Aids Branch who supplied information concerning experiments with films, officials in the educational system of the city of Toronto who kindly permitted certain illustrations and information to be used in this volume, together with the staff of the Saturday Morning Classes for Gifted Adolescents sponsored by the Ontario Department of Education who reported on the subject of gifted pupils. Thanks must also be offered to inspectors and principals of schools, directors and supervisors of art departments and teachers connected with both elementary and secondary schools in the Province who submitted work for appraisal, provided items for illustrative purposes and who allowed the investigators to do research work in their schools and classrooms. Finally, one must thank the pupils who participated in a variety of ways in this endeavour and who produced the art work illustrated in this book.

CONTENTS

CHAPTER   PAGE

    INTRODUCTION v

    LIST OF ILLUSTRATIONS xi

I. RELATING AN ART PROGRAMME TO THE REQUIREMENTS OF ADOLESCENTS . . 1

    1. Some Characteristics of Adolescent Development Affecting Art Education.
    2. Some Modifications in Adolescent Behaviour in Art as a Result of Maturation.
    3. Some Objectives in Developing a Programme of Art Education for Adolescents.
    4. Summary.

II. PROVIDING ACCOMMODATION FOR THE ART ACTIVITIES OF ADOLESCENTS .   8

    1. Factors Affecting Plans.
    2. Specific Considerations in Planning Accommodation.
    3. Summary.

III. TEACHING METHODS RELATED TO AN ART PROGRAMME FOR ADOLESCENTS . . 16

    1. Research into Teaching Methods.
    2. Qualifications of the Teacher.
    3. Clues to a Teaching Method Found in Traditional Art Practice.
    4. The Specific Functions of Art Teachers.
    5. Planning a Programme of Studies.
    6. Grading Output.
    7. Summary.

CHAPTER	PAGE
IV. DEVELOPING THE ADOLESCENT'S APPRECIATION OF HIS ARTISTIC HERITAGE .	35

    1. Means of Developing Appreciation of Art.
    2. Using Films and Filmstrips.
    3. Using Museums and Art Galleries.
    4. Teaching History of Art.
    5. Studying Pictures.
    6. Summary.

V. DESIGN EXPERIENCES FOR ADOLESCENTS .	45

    1. Design in Art and Education.
    2. Approaches of Adolescents Towards Design.
    3. Opposing Methods of Teaching Design.
    4. Pragmatic Approach to the Principles of Design.
    5. Ideas Requiring Generalization.
    6. Activities Placing Emphasis Upon Specific Elements of Design.
    7. Summary.

VI. PICTURE-MAKING BY ADOLESCENTS .	69

    1. The Nature of Picture-Making.
    2. Some Trends in Adolescent Picture-Making.
    3. Some Experiments Related to the Continuity of the Picture-Making Programme.
    4. Some Characteristics of Picture-Making by Adolescents at Various Stages of Development.
    5. Characteristics of Picture-Making Influenced by the Sex of the Adolescent.
    6. Picture-Making by Gifted Adolescents.
    7. Summary.

CHAPTER	PAGE
VII. A PROGRAMME OF OPTIONAL ART ACTIVITIES FOR ADOLESCENTS	97

    1. Research into Optional Activities.
    2. Some Factors Affecting the Choice of Optional Activities.
    3. Guidance of Pupils Working at Optional Activities.
    4. Developing Original Patterns and Designs.
    5. Optional Activities for Individual Work.
    6. Optional Group Activities.
    7. Summary.

CONCLUSION 114

LIST OF ILLUSTRATIONS

PLATE   PAGE

1. Layout and furniture of an art room . . . 9
2. Plan of a general classroom converted to an art room 11
3. A converted classroom featuring sectional furniture for art activities 12
4. Teachers studying in the studio of an artist . 18
5. Young artists attending a seminar in education . 20
6. "Neighbourhood Houses" — a pen-and-ink drawing 28
7. Designing a stage set for "A Midsummer Night's Dream" 30
8. A three-minute pen-and-ink sketch of a living model 33
9. "December" from Chapman's film, "The Seasons" 37
10. "Momentary Hesitation by Railroad Builders" from the National Film Board of Canada production, "Romance of Transportation" . . 38
11. "Masks of the Great Spirits" from the Crawley film, "The Loon's Necklace" 40
12. "Seeing my Baby Sister for the First Time"—a painting in tempera 47
13. Examples of pottery by pupils in middle adolescence 51
14. Making a piece of mobile sculpture . . . 53
15. Weaving on a floor loom 54
16. Three-dimensional geometric design . . . 57

LIST OF ILLUSTRATIONS

PLATE   PAGE

17. A STUDY OF SPACE AND TONES OF GREY, WITH ONE COLOUR ADDED 58
18. A "POINT AND LINE" DESIGN 60
19. NON-OBJECTIVE SCULPTURE IN PLASTER OF PARIS . 61
20. MONTAGE WITH CUT PAPER AND COLOURED INKS . 63
21. WORKING AT THE POTTER'S WHEEL 64
22. NON-OBJECTIVE DESIGN IN TEMPERA 66
23. THREE-DIMENSIONAL ORGANIZATION IN COLOURED PLASTICS 67
24. "GLENNA'S WEDDING"—A PAINTING IN TEMPERA . 71
25. "THE ACCIDENT"—A PAINTING IN TEMPERA . . 73
26. "SLUM CLEARANCE"—A DRAWING IN TEMPERA . . 74
27. "WINDOW CLEANING"—A PAINTING IN TEMPERA . 76
28. "SPRING CLEANING"—A PAINTING IN TEMPERA . . 78
29. "SKETCH IN THE CLASSROOM"—A WASH DRAWING IN WHICH WATER-COLOUR WAS USED 80
30. "ONE MINUTE TO NINE"—A PAINTING IN WATER-COLOUR 84
31. "NOON-HOUR WHISTLE"—A PAINTING IN TEMPERA . 88
32. "MILKWEED"—A PAINTING IN TEMPERA . . . 91
33. "STILL-LIFE PAINTING IN OILS" 94
34. NON-OBJECTIVE SCULPTURE IN WOOD 99
35. PAPER SCULPTURE INVOLVING A MEASURED LINE . . 100
36. LINOLEUM BLOCK-PRINTING ON TEXTILE . . . 103
37. OBJECTIVE PAPER SCULPTURE 105
38. "WILSON'S SNIPE"—A WORK IN WATER-COLOUR AND INK 110
39. MANIPULATING MARIONETTES IN PREPARATION FOR A SHOW 112

CHAPTER I

RELATING AN ART PROGRAMME TO THE REQUIREMENTS OF ADOLESCENTS

1. Some Characteristics of Adolescent Development Affecting Art Education

A PROGRAMME OF ART EDUCATION FOR YOUNG PEOPLE MUST BE governed by the characteristics and requirements of the age group concerned. Adolescence is accompanied by a number of particular problems associated with characteristic physical, intellectual and emotional changes, and demanding modified educational treatment as the pupil develops.

Adolescence is perhaps most remarkable for its peculiar sequence and startling velocity of physical growth. This growth pattern, beginning in the case of girls from eight to twelve years of age, and for boys from nine to thirteen, is unlike anything which has occurred in their lives before and is dissimilar from anything which may come later. It lasts from between four and one-half years to seven and one-half years and is usually complete between the fifteenth and eighteenth years in the case of girls, and between the seventeenth and twentieth years for boys. It is evident that a considerable variation exists between adolescents regarding the ages between which this period begins and ends.

Physical development of individuals occurs in fits and starts and not as an even progression. The period of most rapid physical growth, however, is between twelve and thirteen years for girls, and fifteen to sixteen years for boys. Some idea of the velocity of growth may be gained from the fact that, although during adolescence there is a lag between increase in muscular strength in relation to increase in muscular mass, boys are twice as strong at eleven as they are at six but· by sixteen their strength has doubled again. Accompanying this

1

remarkable development pattern is the attainment of sexual maturity so that many of the problems of adolescence may be said to arise from a source which is endocrine.

The unevenness in the matter of physical development to be found in individual adolescents tends to cause some anxieties to those passing through this period. Boys, for example, may worry over shortness of stature; girls may be disturbed over sexually inappropriate appearance, while facial appearance often causes concern to both sexes. That differences in physical appearance are normal to people in general does not always occur to adolescents. Partly as a result of this preoccupation with deviations in appearance, the adolescent indicates his dislike of being different from his fellows. The tendencies of young people in this age group to affect similar ways of dressing, speaking and behaving are well known. This attitude of conforming to group behaviour creates particular problems for the teacher of art, because in art the individuality of the creating person is of great importance. Actually adolescents are individually very dissimilar as one may quickly observe in art production if a teacher has been successful. One of the chief problems of the art teacher is to find ways and means of helping the pupils to be personal and original in their art activities.

Of further concern to teachers of adolescents is the matter of muscular co-ordination. At the onset of adolescence, physiological growth in some cases retards certain types of co-ordination and agility. The resulting clumsiness demands an extra spaciousness of accommodation in the art class so that accidents with various media may be kept at a minimum and the resulting embarrassments to the young people may, as far as possible, be eliminated. It is obvious, not only that a pupil's inability to meet motor requirements successfully affects his art production directly, but also that because of embarrassment resulting from his clumsiness his output may be adversely affected from an emotional standpoint.

Since adolescence is a period of fluctuating ability in motor control, it would be of assistance to the teacher of art to be able to recommend that only certain tools and materials should be used at specified ages. Art activities, however, are of a general inclusive nature which forbids too much restriction in this regard. Moreover, throughout the adolescence of both boys and girls there are no clearly defined age periods when their motor development either improves or degenerates significantly enough to warrant the recommendation that individuals should start to acquire any particular skill in the use of tools and art materials before or after any given age. Indeed, the idea of a general motor ability is open to question in view of the fact that motor skills are specific. Although the problems associated with the development of motor skill must be treated individually, since girls and boys at any similar period of development exhibit approximately equal motor skill, the whole problem remains uncomplicated by the sex of the pupil. Some variations occur in art production as a result of difference in sex, however, and are to be found in such aspects of the work as the choice of subject matter, the selection of a viewpoint of expression and the development of technique.

A further cause of emotional instability during adolescence may be attributed to the fact that with many individuals physical development and intellectual ability do not keep pace with each other. The pupil may find himself with the physical body and bodily drives of an adult while his mental attitudes remain those of his childhood. Having the outward appearance of an adult, he is not infrequently expected to behave in a manner consistent with his appearance. In the art classes one may sometimes find the most immature expressions produced by a pupil of relatively mature appearance. Since art is an expression of personality such forms must be accepted. To reject them, as was sometimes the case in the past, served only to upset the pupil and hence to retard whatever progress he might have made as he slowly developed mentally. To expect standards of behaviour beyond the capabilities of a pupil is to demand the impossible.

Sometimes a pupil may develop his critical faculties far in advance of his ability to produce art forms. His developing intellectual powers may allow him to gain insights into art and to appreciate work which is much beyond his own standards of production. In contrasting his work with that of others, this pupil may tend to overlook whatever praiseworthy qualities his own work may exhibit. It is with cases of this kind that the teacher must provide the most sensitive and timely guidance, so that the pupils may develop the skills they require in order to achieve such standards of production as will satisfy them.

All human beings are dominated from birth by a number of motives or drives. Included among them are those which prompt us to establish satisfactory relationships with other people and to understand and to master our social environment. During adolescence the individual becomes increasingly aware of self and it is then that these drives take on an added and more consciously personal significance. The skills required to discover and to maintain a satisfactory place in the social environment must, like other skills, be learned and their mastery comes comparatively slowly. During the period in which these skills are being acquired, the pupil sometimes finds himself in situations, particularly those involving both sexes, with which he has not yet learned to cope, with the result that he feels insecure and incompetent. To compensate for such feelings and perhaps to provide himself with a sense of independence, he may resort to petulant behaviour and to acts of bravado. That such forms of behaviour are not acceptable to his associates is manifest, but what is not always so apparent is the fact that behaviour of this kind is rarely satisfactory to the pupil himself. While pupils who act in this way create various problems for an art teacher, they also provide him with opportunities to use art as a most practical means of therapy. The basic subject matter of art revolves around the relationships of the individual to his environment. Furthermore, the expressive acts associated with art demand of the creating person a harnessing and directing of emotions and of intellect. In a suitable programme of art education youth may find practical themes of absorbing personal interest together with positive, creative channels for his energies in the disciplined acts of artistic expression.

2. Some Modifications of Adolescent Behaviour in Art as a Result of Maturation

The six years of research upon which this book is largely based disclosed a number of trends in adolescent behaviour having marked effect upon the pupils' art activities. These trends will be noted only briefly at this time since they will be discussed again in some detail in subsequent chapters. At certain stages, the young person's behaviour may fluctuate between that of childhood and adulthood. The art produced during one week may show signs of some maturity of expression, while during the next it may exhibit many of the characteristics of children's work. The attitudes of many adolescents towards art activities are often unpredictable. Today the young person may "like art"; tomorrow he may have changed his opinion. Sometimes he is aggressive and will assume leadership in group work such as puppetry or mural-making; later he may be timid and retiring. He may alternate between periods of laziness in which he makes little or no attempt to produce art forms, and those in which he works ardently and with deep concentration. His expressive acts may be governed by rational action, or just as readily they may fail because of apparently foolish and irrational behaviour.

If the young person is able to enjoy the benefits of a well-planned and conducted programme of art education, his behaviour in the art class and his art output tend to be more consistent in character. As time goes on his regressions into childlike forms of expression appear less frequently and his work shows a greater self-confidence. Certain developments of an intellectual nature make themselves apparent in his endeavours. With increase in age and because of worthwhile experience, he tends to improve in his ability to realize his intellectual capabilities. If educational conditions are right, this improvement may continue until the end of his school career. Judging from the intellectual content of much of the art production of young people, a period of full intellectual realization is attained later than the middle teens, and may not reach a maximum of attainment until eighteen or nineteen years of age. Because many pupils terminate their art education before they attain full intellectual power, their artistic potentialities, which depend to no small extent upon intellectual endeavour, may never be realized either by their teachers or themselves.

As a result of his increasing achievement, the pupil in later adolescence tends toward greater specialization in his art activities. His selection of activities and the point of view expressed by means of them become more discriminating. Interests become increasingly specific and it is during this period that the emergence and development of vocational interests in art may occur.

Provided with a continuous and efficient programme of art education, older pupils may be expected to show a more consistent pattern of behaviour in their artistic endeavours. An increased use of logical analysis and emotional control, the exercise of considered judgment and taste and the practice of objective self-criticism may be expected as adolescence reaches its final stages.

As personality develops and is expressed by means of art forms, one outstanding fact remains. A study of both the art output and the behaviour of the pupils responsible for it leads to the conclusion that there appears to be no clear cut, typical, or universal pattern of either adolescent behaviour or art production. To work with these pupils in the art class is to work with individuals.

3. Some Objectives in Developing a Programme of Art Education for Adolescents

It has been shown in this chapter that adolescence is a period in which youth is engaged in a struggle to reach maturity. To help the pupils in achieving this goal would appear to be the chief objective of any programme of art education. Accommodation must be provided so that the learners may adjust themselves as readily as possible to the changes resulting from physical growth. A programme must be devised and a pedagogy employed so that the pupils may improve in their ability to reach decisions, to take responsibility and to think objectively. Their art education must also help them to overcome tensions and to employ feeling in expressive acts of a constructive nature. Finally, it must assist young people to understand the society in which they live and to find a satisfactory place in it. In sum, the objectives of art education must include those of assisting adolescents to develop first, an organized pattern of personality and second, a reasonably consistent philosophy of life including a system of values going even beyond those of an aesthetic character.

What are the most favourable conditions and practices in

an art programme which will contribute at all stages of adolescent development to the fulfilment of these objectives? The remaining chapters of this book will discuss this problem from a number of standpoints. The next chapter offers some ideas concerning suitable accommodation for the art activities. Chapter III outlines a system of pedagogy considered to be effective in terms of the functions stated above. Chapter IV discusses the means by which a pupil may learn to appreciate his heritage of art; Chapter V deals with design experiences which may be of value to these students; Chapter VI, with a picture-making programme for these young people, and Chapter VII with a programme of optional art activities.

4. Summary

The sequence of physical, intellectual, emotional and social developments peculiar to adolescents demands especially careful planning of an art programme for this age group. The programme must be conducted largely for the benefit of individuals since each pupil differs from his fellows both physiologically and with regard to personality.

Art education may provide not only personal satisfactions to the pupils, but also therapeutic values to those who suffer from emotional tensions. The outstanding function of a programme of art education for adolescents must be to assist these young people to arrive at a well-balanced maturity.

ADDITIONAL READING:

    Luella Cole. *Psychology of Adolescence.* New York: Farrar and Rhinehart, Inc., 1936.

    Luella Cole. *Attaining Maturity.* New York: Farrar and Rhinehart, Inc., 1944.

    Karl C. Garrison. *The Psychology of Adolescence.* New York: Prentice-Hall, Inc., 1941.

CHAPTER II

PROVIDING ACCOMMODATION FOR THE ART ACTIVITIES OF ADOLESCENTS

1. Factors Affecting Plans for Accommodation

IN ORDER TO SPONSOR AN ADEQUATE PROGRAMME OF ART education for adolescents, the school must provide special accommodation for this purpose. Now that art education embraces a wide scope of activities involving the use of many materials and techniques and in view of the fact that these pupils, because of their rapid physical development, experience a number of motor difficulties, a standard classroom does not permit the most efficient teaching of art at this level.

A survey was made in four countries in which some 60 rooms, either designed primarily to accommodate art or remodelled from regular classrooms for the purpose, were studied.[1] Particular note was made of the location of these rooms in the school buildings, the size of the rooms, the lighting control and electrical outlets provided, the arrangements for washing, the floor coverings, the storage spaces and the display facilities. The comments and recommendations to be found in this chapter are based both upon these observations and upon some local experimentation with designs for art rooms and their furniture.

It was found that art rooms vary greatly from one school to another. One might expect this to be the case since the accommodation must be determined according to several factors. These factors include such items as the numbers of pupils to be accommodated, the activities to be conducted and the budget available.

Frequently an art teacher, either with or without the help of a committee, is asked to make plans to convert a standard classroom into one in which art may be taught. In such cases budgets are often limited. To add to the difficulties of those

[1] Survey made by the Director of Art, Ontario Department of Education, during 1950-51, in parts of England, France, U.S.A., and Canada, in which particular attention was given to newly constructed art accommodation.

PROVIDING ACCOMMODATION FOR ART ACTIVITIES

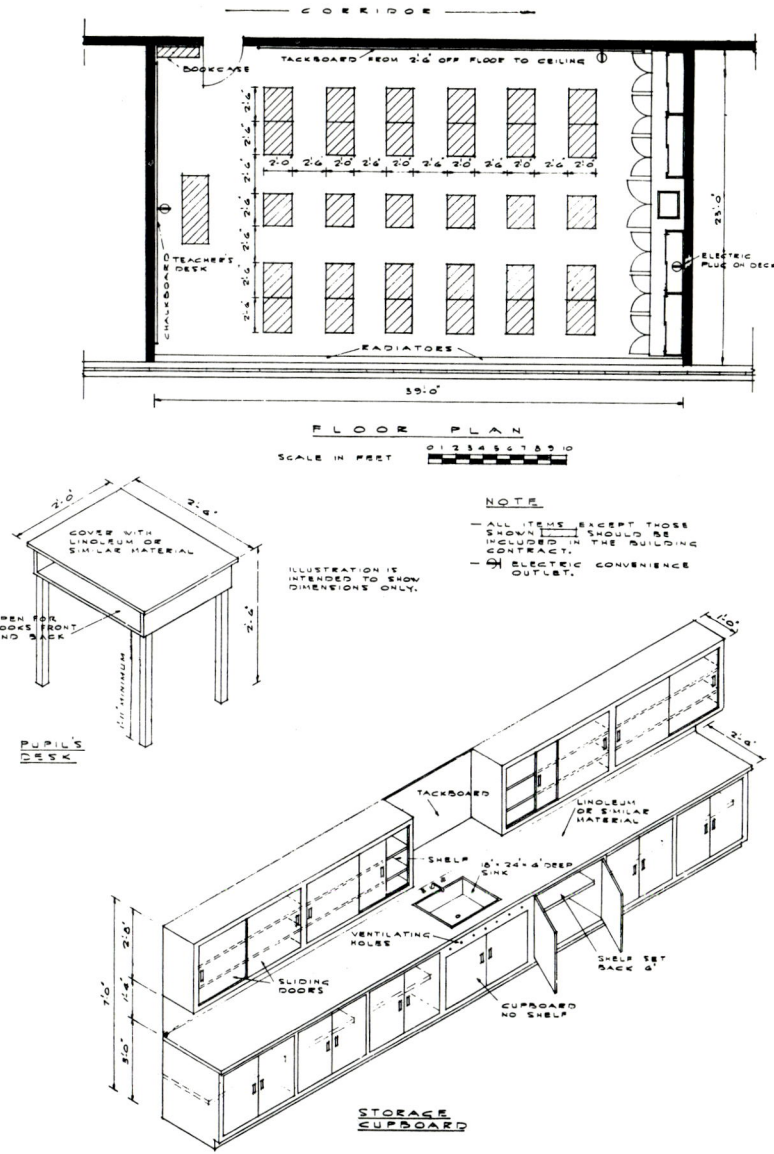

1 Layout and furniture of an art room showing minimum basic accommodation. (Drawing courtesy of the Office of the Technical Adviser, Ontario Department of Education).

planning the reconstruction, there is often the problem in smaller schools in particular of designing a classroom in which one or more other subjects may be taught. These problems can be solved, however, and if the resulting plan is not all that may be desired, a studio-workshop for many art activities can be devised. If all branches of art work cannot be undertaken in such rooms, at least a reasonably broad programme of studies may be planned.

Plate 1 illustrates what may be considered minimum basic accommodation for an art programme for adolescents. These plans are the result of considerable experimentation and have proved themselves practical in the matter of accommodating both art and other classes. They have the added merit of providing suitable but not elaborate accommodation at reasonable cost. The classroom contains some storage space, a sink, some electrical outlets and some display space. At the same time, sufficient blackboard space has been provided both for academic subjects and for some aspects of the teaching in art. The movable desks may be grouped in various positions according to the art or academic activities in progress. The floor space, while not large, has been found adequate for many basic art activities.

Another general classroom which was converted to an art room may be seen in Plate 3. Here it was possible to set apart an area for work with clay and perhaps with some other three-dimensional materials. (See Plate 2.) The desks in the main area are the result of much planning and testing. They have the advantages first, of being sectional and hence readily movable and second, of providing extra storage space for tools, paper and other equipment and supplies.

Very elaborate, attractive and convenient art rooms may be seen in some schools in which large budgets were available for such accommodation. These rooms vary considerably in size, in the general disposition of fixtures and in the equipment provided. The variety to be found in art rooms indicates that no standard pattern may safely be prescribed but that the teacher, the architect and any others concerned must consider the planning of an art room as a creative project to be designed to suit local conditions.

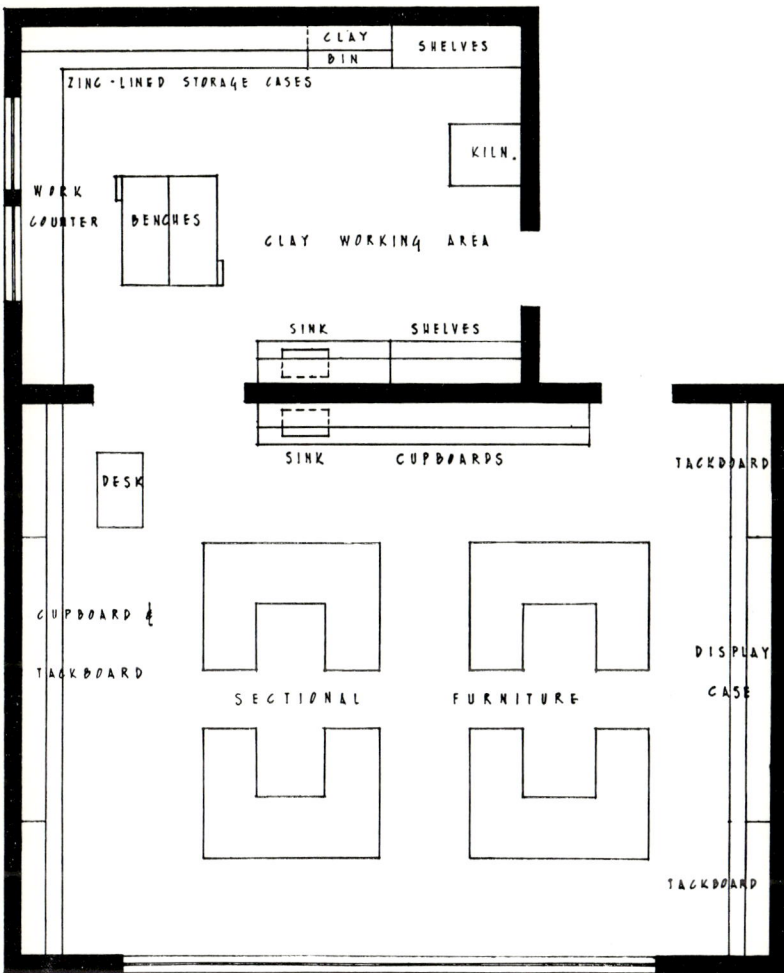

2 Plan of a general classroom which was converted to an art room. An adjacent storage cupboard was included to provide a work area for ceramics. (Plan used by courtesy of the Art Department, Toronto Board of Education).

2. Specific Considerations in Planning Accommodation

Whether a new room is to be designed, or an old one remodelled, several important items must be considered so that the new accommodation may reach a maximum of efficiency. A discussion of some of the most important of these items follows.

3 A converted classroom featuring sectional furniture for art activities. (Photograph courtesy of the Teaching Aids Centre, Toronto Board of Education. Desks designed by the Supervisor of Art, Toronto).

Location in the school building.

To avoid having to move the bulky supplies an undue distance, it is convenient to place the art room on the first floor of a building. If possible, the room should face north so that the natural light will remain relatively constant. In the case of a room not planned to include equipment and tools for work with materials such as wood, metal and textiles, it would be wise to have it situated as close as possible to industrial art shops and home economics rooms. The pupils studying art might then be able conveniently to transfer from the art room to another better equipped for certain activities.

Size of room.

Art teachers have never been known to complain that a classroom was too large. Some of the more costly rooms have been planned to provide a minimum of 40 square feet per pupil. Because of cost, a smaller area than this is usually found. Many practical and reasonably convenient art rooms measure about 25 by 40 feet. Obviously a convenient size will vary, as mentioned previously, according to the enrolment in the classes using the room and in the number and types of activities to be found in the programme of studies.

Lighting control.

The art room requires artificial lighting of high intensity. Light as intense as 40 to 50 foot-candles is not too much for some types of work. Artificial light should approximate the colour of daylight so that the pigments in use remain true in colour under all lighting conditions. Lighting should be distributed so that a minimum amount of shadow is cast.

Since films and film-strips are frequently used in art teaching today, it is convenient to have the room equipped for projection. This necessitates the installation of blackout curtains which may be drawn across the windows.

Electrical outlets.

The type of wiring and electrical outlets installed, whether heavy duty or standard, will depend upon the kinds of equipment the teacher plans to use. Such equipment as kilns and power tools cannot usually be plugged into 110-volt service. The right wiring and outlets must therefore be decided early in the planning of the room to avoid disappointment or heavy extra cost later.

Sinks.

A sink is a necessary piece of equipment in an art room and it should be readily accessible. Some art rooms have a circular sink placed in the middle of the room so that as many as ten pupils may use it at once. This is a costly arrangement and it can be used only in exceptionally large rooms. Plate 1 shows a reasonably convenient and inexpensive placement for a sink. It should be especially noted that a corner location for a sink, because of its inaccessibility, should be avoided. Both hot and cold water should be provided and the sink, the minimum measurements of which should approximate 18 inches by 24 inches by four inches deep, should be surrounded by a waterproof material. The shelf above the sink in Plate 1 is designed to prevent upward splashing.

Floor covering.

In order to eliminate as much noise as possible the floor of the art room should be laid with linoleum or linoleum tile. Linoleum is also practical because it is easy to keep clean.

Storage space.

An art teacher requires storage space for three types of objects: the tools and materials currently in use; the partly completed work of the pupils; and a reserve of tools and materials. An ideal situation is to provide the room first, with many cupboards equipped with adjustable shelves where the materials in use may be stored and in addition, to have a small room adjoining the art room where reserve materials may be kept. Unfortunately, a small storage room adds phenomenally to the cost of the art accommodation. The desks shown in Plate 3 provide some additional storage space, especially for wet work which is always a problem at the end of an art period.

In the matter of small items of equipment such as scissors, paint brushes and knives, the teacher must devise storage methods by which he may quickly check the return of each item. This may be done by providing blocks of wood in which holes have been drilled for the pupils to place pieces of equipment. An empty space may then be easily noticed and the class told of the missing item. Racks for larger objects such as hammers may be used in the same fashion. It might be noted here that the teacher must pay the greatest attention to orderly housekeeping in the art room for a bohemian disorder cannot exist if efficiency is to be maintained in an art programme. The pupils themselves, of course, should take a large part of the responsibility of caring for the room and its contents.

Gas

Should a programme be planned to include activities requiring special heating equipment such as jewellery making or enamel work, a supply of gas must be available.

Display Facilities

Facilities for the display of the art output of pupils should be provided both in the art room and elsewhere in the school. Glass cases as well as display boards should be placed in the halls of the school in order that all pupils may become familiar with the work produced by the art classes. Available wall space in the art room should be covered with display board. The materials used for such board may be selected from various commercially prepared sheets or from soft plywood. In some parts of the room, shelves might be reserved for the display of three-dimensional objects.

To devise attractive and original arrangements for the display of art work should be the duty of the pupils, just as much as the care of the furnishings and tools. The study of display techniques should be considered an art activity of considerable importance and displays should be frequently changed so that interest in them may be kept at a high level. The best spokesman for an art programme in any school is an arresting display of original work.

3. Summary

The planning of art accommodation for adolescents must be considered a creative activity in which several factors related to the pupil enrolment expected, the activities planned and the finances available must be taken into consideration. Art rooms vary, therefore, from one situation to another and no standard formula for the room itself nor for its furniture and equipment can be supplied. The characteristics of physical growth peculiar to adolescents must be taken into consideration whenever plans for art accommodation are being made.

Chapter III

TEACHING METHODS RELATED TO AN ART PROGRAMME FOR ADOLESCENTS

1. Research into Teaching Methods

Research conducted for the purpose of discovering the most effective teaching procedures in an art programme depends upon highly subjective methods of analysis. An investigation, nevertheless, was made in which 219 classrooms were visited where art was being taught to adolescents. In these classrooms careful note was made of each teacher's professional qualifications, the methods he employed, the attitudes of the pupils towards the studies and the art work they produced. The classrooms visited in connection with this study were all within the Ontario educational system and were situated in all geographical regions of the Province.

It was discovered that the qualifications of the teachers varied from attendance in an art class during a year of general studies in a teachers' college, to four years' attendance at a college of art together with an additional year at a teachers' college. Many teachers had also spent three or four summer sessions in studying art.

All manner of teaching methods were observed. Some teachers believed in rigid methods of a dictatorial nature so that a theme might be set without reference to the pupils' experiences. In such classes formal lessons were presented at regular intervals and the pupils later completed exercises upon the themes set by the teachers. Media in these classes were restricted to one type such as water-colour or pencil for all pupils. Often photographic delineations by the pupils of objects drawn with great attention to technique were to be seen. In a few cases, the teachers drew designs upon the blackboard and these the pupils copied. When the history of art was taught it was presented in strict chronological order without reference to the manual work engaging the pupils.

Some teachers, on the other hand, conducted their classes in an entirely different manner. In these classes the pupils were allowed almost complete freedom in their choice of subject matter, together with a very broad choice of media. Often the teacher did not provide a discussion of the topics for expression but instead told the pupils to paint anything that appealed to them. Apparently formal lessons were not given; in fact, it appeared that art lessons of any kind were rarely in evidence.

In other classes the teachers paid particular attention to several teaching devices. It was noted that these teachers gave varying degrees of attention to motivation and to providing some choice of media. Likewise, they allowed different degrees of freedom regarding the points of view expressed by the pupils and the designs they employed to express them. Guidance was usually offered, but it ranged from formal lessons having connection with the work under consideration, to incidental remarks whenever the teacher sensed a need for comment. Some teachers emphasized what they called a "craft" programme while others laid stress upon picture-making. A few teachers allowed the pupils to elect within certain limits their own programmes of studies. Different methods of marking and grading of the art output were observed. In some cases only a general comment was given at the end of a term. In others, each piece of work was allotted a numerical rating to be added to a grand total at the close of the school year. Upon this total a pupil was "passed" or "failed". Further differences of approach on the part of teachers were observed but the above comments will serve as illustrations of the variations one may find in art teaching today.

The differences in the attitudes of the pupils towards their work, together with the work they produced, afforded considerable insight into the effectiveness of the teaching methods observed. Attitudes ranged from consistent boredom and passive submission, to interest and willing participation. The standards of work spread from trite and uninteresting work which resembled the products of uninspired mass production, to output having upon it the stamp of each pupil's personality and other qualities of art.

As a result of these observations, a number of recommendations concerning the qualifications of art teachers and the teaching methods by which they appear to achieve the most beneficial results are set down in the remainder of this chapter.

4 Teachers studying in the studio of an artist. These graduates of Ontario teachers' colleges are gaining skills in art under the guidance of an internationally known painter. Each summer, some 500 Ontario teachers study **art.**

2. Qualifications of the Teacher

A teacher's work is to teach. This applies to all subject fields whether mathematics, English, music or art. In some quarters an idea became prevalent that although the teacher had an important role to play in the teaching of most subjects, where art was concerned it would be better to let the learners go their own way. Where this attitude has prevailed, nothing has proved worse for pupils or for art. The truth of the matter is that the most frustrated learners and those who consequently build up the greatest resistance to art, are the adolescents who are allowed continually without guidance to muddle about with art media. Teaching of the right kind does not inhibit the actions and attitudes of a learner; quite the reverse is true. The teacher who performs his proper function begins to teach young people when first they enter his classroom and continues to teach as long as they remain with him. Neglect anywhere along the line of a pupil's educational career serves to handicap him at the time of neglect and frequently later. The kind of teaching which will suit the adolescent is, therefore, a question of great importance.

Before the question of teaching methods can be discussed, it is necessary to mention the qualifications which a teacher must possess in order to do justice to the important task of conducting an art programme for adolescents. Because a man is an artist is no guarantee that he may successfully teach art; because another is a teacher of other subjects, he may not automatically consider himself equipped to teach this subject.

The successful art teacher of adolescents must have most of the insights and at least some of the capabilities expected of an artist. Certainly he should be able to perform in art to the extent of producing work in both two and three dimensions of a reasonably high standard, since these capabilities tend to provide him with the necessary insights into the true nature of creative activity in the arts. His knowledge of design must be profound and his taste sensitive. He must have an intimate knowledge of mankind's heritage of artistic endeavour. Since the arts are a reflection of men's thinking during any era, it is advisable for the teacher to enjoy a knowledge of the religious, political, philosophical and other historical trends which are manifest in many works of art. The Grecian "orders" of architectural column and the changes wrought on them in the centuries after 400 B.C. by the Romans and others can be appreciated, for example, only in terms of the societies responsible for them. The reasons for the restraint seen in religious sculpture of the thirteenth century compared with the exuberance of the religious paintings produced during the height of the Renaissance can be grasped only by reference to the times in which they appeared. To realize the significance of the expressions of Siqueiros, one must know something of the powerful, if wrong-headed political movements which swayed him, and of the primitivism of the society he reflects. In order to understand a painting by Watteau one should be conversant with the eroticism and elegance of the *Grand Siècle*.

5 Young artists attending a seminar in education. These people who possess many artistic skills are attending a summer school in art in which they are studying pedagogy under the guidance of an expert in educational matters.

As well as qualifying in artistic and historical matters, the teacher must also enjoy the usual professional insights and skills related to the art of teaching. In addition he must possess a particular liking and sympathy for adolescents and he must have given special study to the psychology pertaining to this age group. Finally he must be well read in the fields of both the philosophy and pedagogy underlying art education. In short, the art teacher must be in the most complete sense an artist-teacher.[1] Very rarely is any other type of person successful with these young people in dealing with artistic matters.

[1] In Ontario, the aim of developing artist-teachers has proved to be a realistic one. Since 1944, experiments have been made in providing suitable forms of art education for teachers-in-service. Reports of experimental work were published in: C. D. Gaitskell, *Art Education in the Province of Ontario*, Toronto: Ryerson Press, 1948. Today, hundreds of qualified and efficient teachers attend summer courses in art upon a voluntary basis. As a result of continued high enrolment at these courses, the Department has been able steadily to demand higher standards with regard to the certification of art teachers. Each year in May, an *Orientation Bulletin* is published by the Department describing in detail the courses for the coming season.

3. Clues to a Teaching Method Found in Traditional Art Practice

Perhaps some of the best clues to an adequate teaching programme for adolescents may be found in the endeavours of artists, both living and dead, who have contributed to the artistic tradition of mankind. Since the learning process experienced by the artist apparently differs in no fundamental respect from that experienced by adolescents engaged in artistic pursuits, the manner in which the artist learns is of importance for teachers of these young people. In many respects an artist may be likened to a youth in his developing stage rather than to adults. Bad educational techniques, ugly environment, or sheer inertia which comes to many people with the passing of years are some of the contributory factors to an all too general blunting of perceptive powers and creative abilities found in adults. Because the artist has trained himself to keep his perceptive powers and creative abilities at a high state of sensitivity and readiness, he tends to differ in these respects from his contemporaries in other walks of life. Youth usually differs little from the artist in the matter of receptivity to new experience or ability to create because young people are normally equipped with a daring, seeking, enquiring mind avid for experience to which it reacts with intensity. Fortunately for teachers these qualities are not yet lost when most adolescents come to school.

Why do reputable men perform artistic acts? They do so apparently because they have a compulsion to say something. An inner stirring of idea, a rush of emotion, a feeling of awe or excitement in the face of man's relationship to his environment are the raw materials of all artistic expression. The motivating force of expression although strong, often causes at its inception only an undisciplined reaction. This nebulous reaction to experience which is to be the basis for expression must be moulded by the intelligence until it becomes ordered and defined. Once stimulated, however, an artist becomes emotionally and intellectually more active as the process of clarification begins. He begins to establish tentative goals usually in the form of mental pictures associated with some completed artistic expression based upon his reaction. Eventually he reaches for some suitable medium of expression such as wood, clay or paint and proceeds to grope towards his goal. As he works, he arrives at a further clarification of his experience by fashioning an aesthetic form. The medium he selects must be both resisting and challenging, and yet paradoxically, sufficiently pliant so that it may be manipulated to express even minor subtleties of human reaction.

It should be noted that as well as establishing tentative goals and subsequently thinking more pointedly about his problems in relation to subject matter and design, the artist's search for suitable media and his eventual experimentation with them help him to clarify ideas for expression. At the same time, consideration of a medium may lead to unfortunate outcomes. Sometimes the artist, like Frans Hals or Lorenzo Bernini at their worst, becomes so absorbed with the technique (the way in which he handles a medium) that he tends to forget he had a communication to make. Then the technique, and not the idea takes paramount position and under such conditions the producer becomes a craftsman and ceases to be an artist. The recent trend towards preoccupation with technique often serves to illustrate that virtuosity for its own sake is a poor substitute for art.

Once they have been stimulated and have set up a goal, however tentative, artists frequently find themselves in the often-described "state of hesitation or doubt" which precedes all thinking and is prerequisite to a creative act. No pattern of behaviour can be recalled from the memory to serve completely as a reliable guide for production of a new work. Any new problem of artistic expression has, of course, some relationship to previous experience. At the same time, it has so many new elements that it becomes what might be called an emergent which is distinct and different from all problems yet faced. To follow a formula is to deny creative endeavour.

With the goal established and the new problems defined, not completely perhaps but in a focus sharp enough to start working upon them, the artist may use many means of obtaining leads to satisfactory solutions. He may resort to a watchful trial-and-error as he manipulates his chosen medium; he may study the efforts of others who have struggled with problems reminiscent of the one in hand; he may sketch several trial compositions; he may talk over the matter with fellow artists and others who are interested; he may return, when this is possible, to the original source of inspiration. Thus he goes about absorbing, judging, sifting, discarding, co-ordinating and imagining as his problem gains point and as its solution comes nearer. If this effort is sustained a new work appears. If sensitivity, good judgment and a general honesty (which presupposes originality) are maintained throughout this process, and if feeling and thought are defined in such a way as to be communicated to some others, the artist has followed his calling to the extent of producing an art form.

It was observed that effective contemporary art education has many elements in common with the age-old process described briefly above and as such it is part of a great artistic tradition. The artist enjoys powers of selection, judgment, insight and the like which have been developed far beyond those normally found in youth. One is led to assume, nevertheless, that the constructive forces urging a human being towards expressive artistic acts are to be found universally in normal adolescents. To deny this statement is not to know young people. It would appear that the teacher who governs his pedagogical procedures broadly according to the traditional process of artistic activity cannot go very far wrong because he is being guided by a function of human beings which occurs almost throughout their entire history on earth. We can readily surmise that early man scratching his marks upon the walls of the Lascaux caves was motivated by forces and guided by principles little different from those at work upon the creating person, adolescent or mature, today.

4. The Specific Functions of Art Teachers

Whereas the teacher may apparently be guided with profit by the traditional processes in artistic endeavour, he cannot leave students, as an artist may be left, to find their own solutions to the problems which surround them. The mature artist knows how and where to look for answers to the many questions arising from his work. The teacher on the other hand must perform certain functions on behalf of his pupils before they can profit from art activities.

Concerning Motivation.

We observed that no artistic act can be forthcoming unless its author has been moved by an experience. Artists travel about and have experiences and so do young people. It must be recognized, however, that while the artist thinks about resolving his experiences into disciplined expressive acts, the pupil often does not. Here then is the first function of a teacher of art. Somehow he must reach into the minds of the students and help them not only to select for expression one or more of their moving and hence significant items of experience, but also to persuade them to set themselves goals in terms of a successfully completed aesthetic act. This technique is called "motivation" in educational circles and it means in art education to make pupils aware that they want to say something by producing an art form. Since experience comes in such helter-skelter fashion, a teacher sometimes finds it necessary for purposes of clarification to manipulate the impact of this experience upon the immature minds of youth. Suitable excursions, for example, are arranged to points of interest where a moving experience is likely to be found. Following the experience a discussion takes place to evaluate the significance of the experience or some aspect of it until excitement over a theme mounts. No matter what screening of experience has been arranged, in all cases the theme for expression arises from a personal experience of each learner. There is no other suitable source of subject matter for either adolescent or artist.

Supplying Media.

To furnish pupils with suitable media creates a second function for a teacher. Whereas the artist can go in search of media and his choice is relatively unlimited, pupils are restricted to whatever material is available in the classroom. Different media appeal to different people. This means that the young person as well as the artist must enjoy as wide a choice as possible so that he may eventually find the one medium which suits his personality as well as the project in hand. The range of classroom materials cannot, for such practical reasons as expense and storage, be as wide as that from which the artist may choose. Nevertheless, the teacher must provide a maximum range of materials consistent with local conditions.

Allowing Freedom for Exploration.

Sometimes a creating person must be left alone. There comes a time in the creative process when experience must be ordered and defined, and this can occur only in and with oneself. At such a time one has many explorations to make; with the materials at one's disposal, with the elements of design and with the thoughts generated by experience. This period is as vital for the adolescent as it is for the adult. Provided with inspiration and materials the young learner, like the artist, must be left alone to come to grips with his problem. The teacher in stepping aside at this point is performing a further necessary function.

Studying Pupils and Their Output.

For those who are interested in the study of personality and this includes in particular teachers of adolescents, observation not only of the art produced but also of the individual giving his energies to artistic creation is revealing. The struggle to express in artistic form a reaction to experience displays many facets of the personality of the creating person. Careful observation of both the art work and the learners who produce it provides teachers with clues as to the types of pupils with which they must associate. It singles out those who are "matter-of-fact" and "down-to-earth" as opposed to those who are poetic and imaginative. It shows those who are bold enough to venture along new paths, those who cling to familiar ways, those who persevere and those who are easily discouraged. It may reveal the potential scientist, the biologist, the developing designer and the craftsman. It tends to disclose the introverted and the extraverted, the brilliant and the mentally handicapped and the normal or the disturbed mind. Careful study of students engaged in art, therefore, is a further function of the teacher. From the clues gained by this observation the teacher, without going so far as to turn himself into an amateur psychologist, may learn to be a sensitive counsellor so that the guidance he may offer will be effective and timely. Nowhere in teaching is guidance of this kind more important than with adolescents.

Offering Guidance.

The guidance of pupils is the most important function in the whole process of their artistic development. One may think of guidance as a pedagogical device having the purpose of assisting the learner to say what he wants to say in the way he wants to say it. Guidance is a device of helping a student towards self-realization through the achievement of his goals. The educational principles associated with guidance are today perhaps the best known and the most abused of all the principles in the entire art of teaching.

The adolescent as well as the artist seeks guidance. The latter is always free to accept or reject whatever guidance he is offered and if he is an honest man he is always governed by an integrity of long standing based upon his ideals and artistic purposes. Freedom of choice and of action are cherished by the artist but it is the teacher who must help in guarding them for the pupil. The persuasive teacher has the power to offer freedoms of thought and action, or he can just as easily deny them. The adolescent is in a vulnerable position for he can be readily persuaded by a skilful teacher to adopt any modes of thought and action approved within the classroom. Dictatorships and democracies alike are formed largely from the malleable material of growing minds. It would appear that the teacher must be constantly alert not to use any form of guidance which would restrict either the idea being expressed or the design used to express it. It is the young learner's right to enjoy freedom in these two respects, for without this freedom artistic expression at any level cannot be realized. The truth of this statement was never made more apparent than in the art of Germany under Hitler, but many other examples involving say, the French Romanticists of the early 1800's or the Fauves at the close of that century will come to mind in which aesthetic dictatorships rather than those of a political and aesthetic nature combined have occurred. Fortunately for art, rebellious spirits from Géricault to Epstein appear in spite of the disapproval of established salons and academies. All this by no means infers that guidance should be passive. Lacking a planned programme of guidance, a pupil may fail to realize as fully as he might the goals which he has set for himself as a result of previous motivation. Ideas and the means of expression (media, technique and design), are the two inseparable aspects of expression in which the adolescent requires strong guidance.

Sometimes the pupil forgets, either wholly or in part, the reaction to experience which he intended to express. In this case the teacher must help him to recall the experience which moved him. Recall may be achieved by arranging a repetition of the experience itself or by questioning him so that his thoughts may return to the original motivation. Sometimes the experience proves to be unsuitable and the pupil must search for other themes. Whether or not the pupil requires any of these forms of guidance may usually be determined by studying his behaviour following motivation. Listlessness or extreme hesitancy, conditions which are not infrequently found during early adolescence in particular, tend to indicate the need for specific teaching measures.

Sometimes guidance must be concerned with tools, materials and techniques. All normal young people wish to experiment with new processes and as has been indicated previously, they should be encouraged to do so. To permit a pupil to experiment with tools and material merely for the purpose of experimentation, however, may lead eventually only to blind alleys or to bad habits unless suitable guidance is forthcoming. Explanation given at the right moment about processes or materials and the way in which they are used for expressive purposes often aids the pupil to accomplish his own task of expression. As will be shown in Chapter IV, visits to art galleries and museums may be particularly valuable in this connection. Sometimes a student will become so engrossed with a technique that he tends to forget his idea for expression. It is then that a teacher must help him to free himself from the domination of technique in the interest of expression. The teacher may find it necessary to supply an entirely new medium to replace the one which is being abused. If a choice must be made between expression and technique, then technique must be sacrificed at least for the time being.

Guidance related to drawing and composition creates problems for teachers of adolescents. Little children strike out fearlessly and will draw or compose without difficulty. It was

6 "Neighbourhood Houses"—a pen-and-ink drawing. An 18-year-old boy has developed a high degree of skill in drawing. He has done so by means of expressive work, and not through dull drills.

stated in the opening chapter that as children enter adolescence they become unsure of themselves while their critical faculties outstrip their abilities to produce art work. It is then they require help in drawing and in developing facility in the use of the elements of design. Then the teacher must be guided by the needs of the learners in relation to expression. Where a need for teaching is apparent without which the learner could not proceed satisfactorily, a lesson must be forthcoming and practice to improve a skill encouraged. The old academic idea that drawing is good discipline and should be engaged in for its own sake is scarcely to be recommended. Sensible artists have perfected their ability in this respect for expressive purpose and not because of academic or *beaux-arts* institutional practices. Sensible teachers must be governed by similar thinking related to adolescents.

Perhaps the most difficult problems to solve in all art teaching are connected first, with the timing of guidance and second, with the amount of guidance to be given. Guidance offered before the learner realizes that he requires help is usually ineffective as a teaching technique. A learner must be personally aware of a problem before its solution can have any real meaning for him so that the teacher may be forced to take time to help pupils clarify their problems before proceeding to other matters. Too much guidance takes away the learner's initiative while too little leaves him unable to proceed in his work. When guidance should be given and how much guidance should be offered must depend upon individual cases and situations. Only the teacher himself can decide and no formula can help him. This freedom of choice of action left to the teacher is a recognition of the fact that teaching is a profession and an art of considerable challenge. It gives point to the statements made earlier to the effect that the teacher must be not only familiar with artistic processes but also creative in his own professional endeavours. By keeping firmly in mind the basic principle that the pupil like the artist must be the controlling participant of the activity in progress, he can adjust his teaching procedures to maintain a delicate balance between necessary leadership on his part and freedom on the part of the pupil. The teacher who believes in maintaining a balance of this kind will never resort to the "pattern" type of teaching so prevalent in the not so distant past. To provide drawings to be copied, drills for the development of facility with various media, or work-kits for painting or craft activities has nothing to do with aesthetic education, affords no vital motivation, offers no real problems, stimulates no real thinking and serves only to remove from the learner the opportunity of profiting from art activities. In other words, these unfortunate so-called educational devices have no connection with artistic tradition.

Some time ago Sir Herbert Read, in speaking before the members of a UNESCO Seminar on art education, gave what he considered to be the functions of aesthetic education. Sir Herbert pointed out that any form of aesthetic education must preserve the natural intensity of all modes of perception and sensation and must co-ordinate the various modes of perception and sensation with one another, and in relation to environment.

7 Designing a stage set for *A Midsummer Night's Dream*. This girl works with great concentration upon an elected activity.

All aesthetic education, said the speaker, must finally lead to the expression of feeling and thought in communicable form. In these comments we have a summary which applies to both artist and adolescent and which may act as a guide to any teacher of art.

5. Planning a Programme of Studies

If the pupils must be treated as the controlling participants of the art activities which engage them, the question might be raised as to whether or not they should have any part in the planning of the programme of studies which they follow. It is well known by those who have contact with adolescents that young people like to have a voice in what they do. It makes very little difference which of the numerous types of art work may be chosen from a long list of activities. There are the two exceptions of picture-making and historical studies (a topic which will be discussed later[1]). Provided that the learner approaches an art activity with the traditional attitudes associated with art, he may engage himself in any artistic work of his choice and still derive the full personal benefits which art has to offer.

[1]*Seq.*, p. 97.

An interesting experiment was conducted with three classes of approximately 25 pupils each.[1] Beginning in the seventh grade and continuing for four years, the pupils were allowed to choose the art activities which interested them most. Because the person in charge of the experiment felt that he could not otherwise do justice to teaching, he limited the number of options available at any time to four. Thus life-drawing, stencilling on textiles, puppetry and mural-making might be available for a specified period, while later still-life painting, silk screen work, a study of local architecture and work in leather might be offered. At the end of the four-year experiment, it was found that the pupils had elected a well-balanced programme of studies which included a good proportion of picture-making, historical studies, three dimensional activities and group work. It must be pointed out that the teacher presented options which would allow a well-balanced programme to be elected. The pupils demonstrated a high degree of interest in their activities and produced art of a commendable standard.

It would appear wise, therefore, to encourage pupils to have a considerable part in planning their programme of art work. To make such planning effective the teacher must place his confidence in his class. While acting as a counsellor, he must be prepared to accept many decisions and choices of action arrived at by the pupils even if at times he does not entirely agree with some of the conclusions reached. In the long run, learning becomes more efficient when pupils can strive to reach the goals which they set for themselves. Fortunately the nature of art lends itself to an almost unlimited freedom of choice on the part of the learner.

6. Grading Output

To pass judgment upon any form of artistic output is one of the most difficult tasks which anyone can undertake. Eminent critics have been proved wrong over geniuses from Beethoven to Hindemith, from Blake to Cézanne. It is not surprising that teachers of adolescents may find themselves in error

[1] An experiment conducted by the Director of Art, Ontario Department of Education, between the years 1940 and 1943 (inclusive), when he was the Art Supervisor of the Powell River and District Schools (British Columbia).

whenever they attempt a quantitative judgment of the work produced in an art class. The difficulty in trying to assign marks or grades to this work lies chiefly in the fact that no two pieces of art are alike and therefore they cannot be compared. Work produced is either art or not art; it lies within a universal artistic tradition or is outside it. The result of an expressive act which is based upon a reaction to personal experience and is presented in terms of an appropriate design lies within the boundary of art. If it fails in any of these respects it resides outside the province of art and belongs in some other field of endeavour. Even confronted with a choice of whether the result of an expressive act is art or not, well informed people have found difficulty in coming to acceptable decisions. Quantitative judgment of the works observed has usually proved to be quite beyond the capabilities of these people.

Attempts have been made from time to time to develop tests to measure the abilities of pupils both to appreciate and to produce art. None of these tests including the *Art Judgment Test* by Meier and Seashore, the *McAdory Art Test* and the *Tests in Fundamental Abilities of Visual Art* by A. F. Laurenz has lived up to the expectations of their makers. All well-known tests of this kind have proved in time to be largely invalid and unreliable.

The teacher of adolescents would be wise in confining himself to an appraisal of the work of each member of his class in terms of whether art has been produced or not. Although even in this task the teacher may at times be in error, he will if he is a sensitive and highly trained person, stand more chances of being correct than if he attempts to grade or to compare the art of his pupils.

A danger arising from an attempt to assign marks or grades to the art production of pupils lies beyond the probable error of the teacher. Any attempts to mark the work of pupils immediately tends to set up a spirit of competition between the members of an art class. A study of the lives of artists from Fra Angelico to Gauguin reveals that almost without exception, those who have succeeded have been concerned more with their own standards of production than with these standards in relation to others. While an artist must continu-

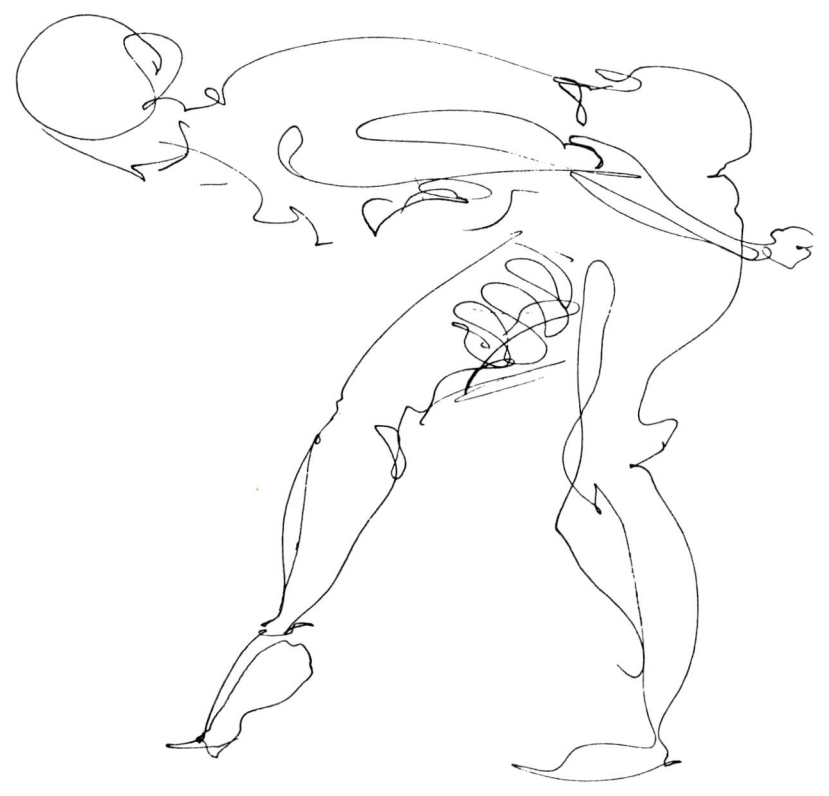

TEACHING METHODS RELATED TO AN ART PROGRAMME 33

8 A three-minute pen-and-ink sketch of a living model by a 17-year-old boy. Is it art? What mark or grade is it worth?

ally try to improve upon his previous achievements, he cannot afford to allow a competitive spirit to enter into his efforts. Once such an attitude occurs his own standard of output tends to deteriorate. One may readily understand why this should be the case by referring once more to the traditional nature of art. Art is one of the means by which men share their thoughts and feelings. It is a medium for an offering of mind and heart from one human being to others. As such it is incompatible with competitive practices.

In conclusion one may say that teachers would be well advised to hesitate before attempting to assign marks or grades to the art production of adolescents. If these young people are attempting in a sincere spirit to produce the best art of which they are capable, both the pupils and the teacher are succeeding in their tasks.

7. SUMMARY

In order to qualify as an art teacher of adolescents, one must achieve competence as both an artist and a teacher. The type of teaching which is being followed successfully in many quarters today in no way departs from the broad principles of an age-old activity belonging to artistic endeavour. Contemporary teaching methods appear to adhere closely to the main principles developed by men throughout the history of creative output. Whenever art education has gone wrong, it seems to have done so because it has run counter to the traditional modes of artistic expression.

The main functions of an art teacher are concerned with the use of motivation based upon personal experience, with providing a wide range of media, with allowing the pupils freedom for the exploration of ideas and techniques, with the careful study of individual pupils and their art output and finally with offering timely and effective guidance.

The pupils should have a voice in planning their programme of study in art and their output should not be subjected to a quantitative system of marking.

ADDITIONAL READING:

Victor D'Amico. *Creative Teaching in Art*. Scranton, Pa.: International Text Book Company, 1942.

Rosabell MacDonald. *Art as Education*. New York: Henry Holt and Company, 1941.

Progressive Education Association. *The Visual Arts in General Education*. New York: D. Appleton-Century Company, Incorporated, 1940.

Herbert Read. *Education Through Art*. London: Saber and Saber, 1943.

Marion Richardson. *Art and the Child*. London: University of London Press, Limited, 1948.

Unesco: Edwin Ziegfeld (Ed.) *Education and Art*. Paris: Unesco House, 19 Avenue Kléber, 1954.

TEACHING PORTFOLIOS:

National Industrial Design Council (Donald W. Buchanan, Editor). *Better Design in Canadian Living*. Ottawa: National Gallery, 1954. (10 portfolio sheets, 11" by 14".)

Museum of Modern Art, *Teaching Portfolios*, Series 1 and 2. New York: Museum of Modern Art (a catalogue is available from the Museum, 11 West 53 Street, New York 19, N.Y.).

Chapter IV

DEVELOPING THE ADOLESCENT'S APPRECIATION OF HIS ARTISTIC HERITAGE

1. Means of Developing Appreciation of Art

THE PRODUCTION OF ART FORMS HAS ENGAGED THE ATTENTION OF men for thousands of years. In art we may find an intimate record of the reactions of men to their environment in every known civilization which has existed on earth. Lacking an understanding of this vast cultural background, no person can be said to be adequately educated. Hence it is of great importance that before students leave school they should have some acquaintance with man's artistic heritage.

To bring to the attention of young people the artistic achievements of mankind, the teacher may resort to the use of films and film-strips; he may take his classes to museums and art galleries within reach and he may give several types of lessons dealing with the history of art. Each of these teaching devices requires thoughtful use and a wide knowledge of the material available. Today, a great wealth of excellent reproductions of works of art in various pictorial forms is readily available. Never before have teachers of art enjoyed equal opportunities to bring to the classroom such a wide selection of appropriate visual aids.

In order to discover ways and means of using visual aids most effectively a number of experiments were conducted with groups of adolescents.[1] Many types of art films and film-strips, numerous reproductions of pictures and other works of art were used with pupils of different ages. These visual aids were employed for various teaching purposes including the development of insight into the art of others, the development of technical facility with tools and materials and as a motivating force for expression. The films, film-strips and reproductions were used at different stages of art lessons. On occasion they

[1]Since 1945, experiments have been conducted within the Ontario educational system by both the Audio-Visual Aids Branch and the Art Branch.

were employed to introduce topics, sometimes they were shown as an aid to teaching a topic and at other times they were used to review work which had previously engaged the attention of pupils. The effectiveness of both the visual aids themselves and the teaching methods employed with them was judged according to the attitudes of the pupils and their art production which had been affected by their observations. The remainder of this chapter outlines some conclusions resulting from this research into the use of visual aids.

2. USING FILMS AND FILM-STRIPS

An increasing use of films, film-strips and other visual aids is to be found in contemporary art education. Their intelligent use can greatly increase the effectiveness of teaching and can broaden the range of subject matter of the art programme. Well chosen visual aids can serve to give point and support to any lesson on art and in particular to those in which the artistic achievements of others are being considered.

In recent years the supply of effective art films suitable for adolescents is becoming more abundant. These films fall into three broad classifications: first, there are the films shown to demonstrate the skills developed by others in their chosen areas of artistic production; then there are the films designed for the development of appreciation which consequently place little emphasis upon technique; and third, there are those not designed as art films, but because of some peculiar property, serve as an inspiration and sometimes even as a motivating force for expression. Some films may fall into all three classifications.

Examples of the first category might include the following: *A.B.C. of Puppet Making* (Bailey); *An Outdoor Mural on the Arts* (Harman); *Drawing to Music* (Crawley's, Ottawa, and International Film Bureau, Chicago). Films of this type vary greatly in their effectiveness. Such a film can never replace the thoughtful and timely instruction of an expert teacher; nor can it substitute for learning gained as a result of experience with material itself. Some films designed to teach skill may actually be harmful if they attempt to present "step-by-step" teaching methods or formulae for the drawing of objects. The

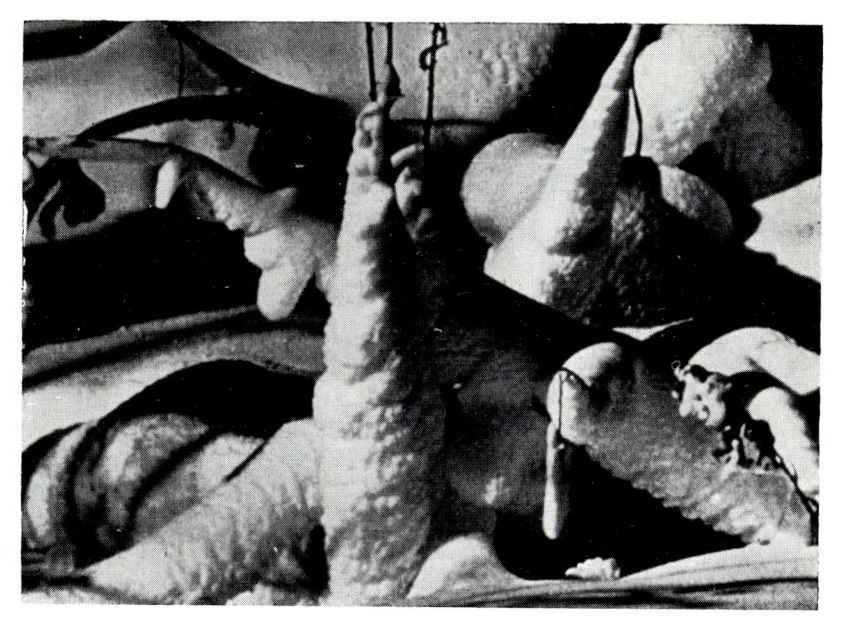

9 "December" from Chapman's film, *The Seasons.* (Photograph courtesy of Imperial Oil Company, Canada).

over-simplifications and distortions shown may serve only to inhibit the learner's observation of his environment and to interfere with his struggle to produce significant and personal design.

Films for further development of skill including those listed above may be most satisfactory. The searching lens of the camera is able to place particular emphasis upon certain aspects of a technique, so that by focussing upon the precise and sensitive actions of an expert, a film may be produced which is both an inspiration and a means of developing skill.

In the second category, those films which tend to develop appreciation of the works of others may be exemplified by the following: *Works of Calder* (Museum of Modern Art Film Library); *Cathedral of Chartres* (Post Pictures Corporation); *Images Médiévales* (A. F. Films Inc.,); *Looking at Sculpture* (Brandon); *Il Demoniaco Nell'Arte* (Film Advisory Centre). By means of such films the pupils may see both two- and three-dimensional art forms which otherwise they might never have the opportunity of observing. Some of the films in this category,

10 "Momentary Hesitation by Railroad Builders," from the National Film Board of Canada production, *Romance of Transportation*. (Photograph courtesy of the producers).

and in particular *Images Médiévales*, are produced with such faultless technique and with such excellent regard for the qualities of work under consideration, that they serve as an acceptable substitute for original works of art which are inaccessible.

In the third category, those films which are not designed as art films but which possess upon completion certain undefined inspirational qualities might include the following: *The Loon's Necklace* (Crawley's, Ottawa, and International Film Bureau, Chicago); *The Seasons* (Chapman for the Imperial Oil Company, Canada); *Begone Dull Care* (McLaren for the National Film Board); *The Romance of Transportation* (National Film Board). Such films were no doubt designed either as instructional material or as entertainment but they all exhibit an art quality which cannot fail to inspire young people. Films in this class appear relatively infrequently, but when they do occur they may be of great value to the teacher of art.

What are the criteria for judging the value of an art film to be shown to adolescents? First, the techniques of film-making employed, both in vision and sound, must be of the highest technical standards. Next, where facts are presented they must be authentic and accurate. Third, the film must do no violence to the expression of the artist. Movement depicted by means of quick shots of various sections of a painting, as shown in *Toulouse-Lautrec*, for example, sometimes develops rhythms remote from those achieved structurally by the painter and seems only to destroy the aesthetic organization of the original work. Fourth, if the film is concerned directly with art education it should allow great scope for the initiative of both teachers and pupils. Fifth, the film must be suitable to the specific level of ability and understanding of its audience. In brief, an art film while conforming to the tenets of an acceptable aesthetic must assist materially in the pupil's education for good taste, for honesty of expression and for the development of his insight into the art forms depicted.

The teacher may use a film for three purposes: to introduce a topic, to assist in the teaching of a topic and to review a topic. It is manifest that the teacher must make careful plans if a film is to be effective in any of these teaching situations. The film must be presented at exactly the right moment in relation to the current problems facing a class. The teacher must be familiar with the film so that he may, when necessary, enlarge upon its teachings, or offer explanations of any obscure or omitted ideas related to the theme. Questions, discussions and written reports may from time to time be necessary in the classroom in order that the pupils may derive maximum benefit from the screening.

Most of the comments concerning films apply equally to film-strips. The film-strip, although lacking the dynamic qualities of movement and sound associated with films, has the one important advantage of allowing the teacher to control its pace of presentation.

3. Using Museums and Art Galleries

The teacher of art who finds himself within reach of a good museum and a good art gallery is fortunate. In these

11 "Masks of the Great Spirits" from the Crawley film, *The Loon's Necklace*. (Photograph courtesy of the producers and of Imperial Oil Company, Canada).

institutions he may make firsthand use of all manner of original works of art. The same careful planning which is necessary in the use of films and film-strips must be observed in visiting a museum or an art gallery. To walk at random through the halls and galleries of these institutions is pleasant enough and practical also for purposes of orientation but little, if any learning takes place under these conditions once the general plan of the institution has become familiar. It is even doubtful if lectures prepared and presented without reference to the work engaging the pupils in school by members of the staff of these institutions are as effective as they might be.

Paintings and other art forms displayed in museums and art galleries should usually be approached by the pupils only when they have specific problems in mind related to the works on view. Unable to discover a specific reason for the expedition which affects him personally, the young person will tend to be bewildered by the vast array of objects confronting him. Lectures about these objects in which he has no personal interest will probably bore him. On the other hand, if he brings with him problems related to some of his previous experiences in art which have been skilfully brought into sharper focus by his teacher prior to the visit, he may quickly learn to appreciate whatever the institution has to show him.

One may observe from time to time groups of young people drawing with meticulous care and photographic reality some of the objects displayed in a museum or art gallery. The wisdom of this practice may be questioned. Although a certain technical skill in drawing may result from such an exercise, it would appear that the skill developed is divorced from original thinking. Pupils might be better employed in studying the work on display in the manner described in the previous paragraph. Any drawing which occurs could take the form of analytical sketches to record the rhythms of lines, the textural qualities seen and felt, the pictorial compositions admired and so on. The museum and art gallery should be used to develop personal vision and insight and not to encourage thoughtless copying or pointless learning.

4. Teaching History of Art

A history of art may be taught by three methods or rather, approaches to the subject: first, by the chronological method; second, by starting at the present and working backwards; and third, by teaching it incidentally in relation to the current activities in the art room.

To teach history according to its chronological sequence is probably for the teacher the safest and easiest approach to the subject. Certainly this is the method used in most history classes. When a history course in art is planned to span three or four school years, it has the very grave deficiency of leaving many pupils who do not continue their schooling into the higher levels ignorant of the important contemporary period. One may discover many such pupils who may be reasonably familiar with the story of man's cultural achievements up to, say the Renaissance, but who know little or nothing of the story of art from that period to the present day.

Teaching history from the present to the past eliminates this difficulty. By this method, examples of contemporary output may be studied and the influences upon the artists in question traced. This method seems to be particularly useful in studying architecture where buildings in the immediate environment often exhibit the influences of the past. The drawbacks of the method lie in the relatively great amount of knowledge and insight which the teacher must possess, and in the careful preparation he must make in organizing his teaching materials and in promoting and guiding research activities.

To teach history incidentally in relation to the work being produced in an art class has much to recommend it on the grounds that it tends to relate the history to a framework of thinking already established by the pupils. The method could be deficient by leaving the class with only a fragmentary knowledge, rather than a broad and integrated understanding of our cultural background.

Tests in the use of each method and a combination of them, together with the observation of many classes in which the various methods were used, form the basis of the following comments and recommendations. It appears that to use a combination of these methods is to be recommended. In the academic history classes of the school it may be assumed that the specialist in history devotes a reasonable portion of his time to a consideration of mankind's cultural development. It is scarcely possible to deal with history in general unless achievements in art are given some attention. In these classes the teaching will no doubt follow the usual method of chronological order of presentation. The other two methods may then be left to the art teacher who, working in close co-operation with the teacher of history, may with his special knowledge and ability enrich the history courses.

Whatever teaching methods are employed, studies in the history of art must not degenerate into a presentation and examination of facts alone. It is also essential that pupils have the opportunity of seeing many original works or, failing that, excellent reproductions of them. To acquire a number of isolated facts about the history of art is like collecting a few worthless coins to jingle ostentatiously in the pocket. The history of art must be taught so that a student acquires not only some of the essential historical facts related to the subject, but also a personal appreciation of the true nature of artistic endeavour throughout the ages.

5. Studying Pictures

Although the subject of picture study has been discussed previously, a few further remarks by way of summary appear necessary. All experiments in connection with picture study by adolescents lead to the conclusion that a study of pictures in which the teacher sets a formal course is generally ineffective. Pupils appear neither to find sufficient interest in a formal study of pictures, nor to gain adequate insights into the works observed under these conditions, to warrant recommending this practice. Only when pictures are studied in connection either with some related manual activities or with some aspect of history arousing the interest and stirring the imagination of a pupil, is this activity educationally efficient.

To teach picture study in an integrated fashion, the teacher must have at his disposal many fine reproductions of collections of works by individual artists. These may be found in several series of publications including the *Penguin* books, the *Skira* books and those published by the Museum of Modern Art in New York. These publications are readily obtainable through many booksellers. Another source of illustrative material may be found in most large art galleries where catalogues are usually available. The teacher who makes some effort should have little difficulty in developing a commendable library of reproductions.

6. Summary

A person cannot be said to be educated who lacks an understanding and appreciation of mankind's artistic heritage. The teacher may make use of films, film-strips, museums and art galleries and good reproductions of original works to develop the adolescent's insight into this heritage. In resorting to any of these means the teacher must be guided by carefully selecting teaching practices. Every teacher of art should develop an excellent library of reproductions.

A history of art may be taught by several methods. Whichever method is used, the pupil must gain a personal insight into the true nature of art and not merely a number of historical facts.

ART EDUCATION DURING ADOLESCENCE

ADDITIONAL READING:
- American Federation of Arts. (William McK. Chapman, Ed.) *Films on Art, 1952.* Kingsport, Tenn.: Kingsport Press, Inc., 1952.
- Eleanor Bitterman. *Art in Modern Architecture.* New York: Reinhold Publishing Corporation, 1952.
- Sheldon Cheney. *The Story of Modern Art.* New York: The Viking Press, 1941.
- Sheldon Cheney. *A World History of Art.* New York: The Viking Press, 1945.
- Paul Duval. *Canadian Drawings and Prints.* Toronto: Burns and MacEachern, 1952..
- Leo Frobenius and Douglas C. Fox. *Prehistoric Rock—Pictures of Europe and Africa.* New York: Museum of Modern Art, 1937.
- Helen Gardner. *Understanding the Arts.* New York: Harcourt, Brace and Company, 1932.
- Lester Morgan. *World Furniture Treasures, Yesterday, Today and Tomorrow.* New York: Museum of Modern Art, 1954.
- Museum of Modern Art. *Modern Architecture in England.* New York: Museum of Modern Art, 1937.
- Beaumont Newhall. *The History of Photography.* New York: Museum of Modern Art, 1949.
- New Educational Library. (Lord Gorell, Advisory Ed.) *The Arts: Painting, The Graphic Arts, Sculpture and Architecture.* London: Odhams Press, Ltd., 1948.
- Nikolaies Peosner. *Pioneers of Modern Design.* New York: Museum of Modern Art, 1949.
- Olive Riley. *Your Art Heritage.* New York: McGraw-Hill, 1952.
- Andrew Carnduff Ritchie. *Sculpture in the Twentieth Century.* New York: Museum of Modern Art, 1952.
- James Johnson Sweeney. *Alexander Calder.* New York: Museum of Modern Art, 1943.
- Monroe Wheeler. *Modern Painters and Sculptors as Illustrators.* New York: Simon & Schuster, 1946.

Magazines.
- *American Artist.* (E. W. Watson and A. L. Guptell, Editors). Watson-Guptell Publications, Inc., 24 W. 40th St., New York 18, N.Y.
- *Canadian Art.* (Robert Ayre and Donald W. Buchanan, Editors). Box 384, Ottawa, Ontario.
- *The Studio.* London: The Studio Ltd., 66 Chandos Place, London W.C. 2, England.
- *School Arts.* (D. Kenneth Winebrenner, Editor). The Davis Press, Inc., Printers' Building, Worcester, Mass.

INFORMATION CONCERNING THE NATIONAL FILM BOARD (OF CANADA)

The National Film Board has offices in each of the Canadian provinces. The address of the Ontario office is as follows: 70 Yorkville Ave., Toronto 5, Ontario.

The National Film Board office in the United Kingdom is located at Colquhoun House, Broadwick Street, London W.1, England; and those in the U.S.A., at 400 West Madison Street, Chicago 6, Illinois; and 1270 Avenue of the Americas, New York 20, N.Y. The Chicago office is for free travel films and information only.

Catalogues are available from the National Film Board, including pamphlets listing current releases.

SOME MAJOR PRODUCERS OF ART FILM-STRIPS:

Curriculum Films; Encyclopedia Britannica; Educational Productions Ltd.; Jam Handy; National Film Board (of Canada); Society for Visual Education; Young America Films.

Chapter V

DESIGN EXPERIENCES FOR ADOLESCENTS

1. Design in Art and Education

DESIGN IS THE STRUCTURE OF AN ART FORM. IT IS THE AESTHETIC organization by means of which a communication is made. One would be wrong to think of design as a separate and distinct field of art. Design cannot be divorced from any artistic expression, because the message conveyed by a work of art is made apparent by means of the design employed. Whenever any art form is being produced a problem of design is automatically involved.

To learn how to create an appropriate design is the result of much experience and of long and careful study. To learn to appreciate fully the style, precision, appropriateness and further excellent qualities to be found in the designs of others requires equal effort. There is no quick method of learning design. Rather, years of controlled experimentation, observation and selective judgment are required before a sure taste and insight may be gained in this field of art education.

To discover the attitudes of adolescents towards design activities, to learn something of the type of designs which these pupils produce and to analyze teaching methods appropriate to this field of art, some research was conducted. Over 200 classrooms were visited while activities involving design were in progress. Later the output of 970 pupils enrolled from the seventh to the twelfth grades was collected for analysis. In all, 2,040 designs in both two and three dimensions were analyzed in terms of their unity and variety and in relation to the elements and materials which the pupils employed. The standards of output were then checked against the types of teaching methods observed in the classrooms. This chapter presents observations and recommendations in the light of this research in Ontario schools.

2. Approaches of Adolescents Towards Design

It was found that as adolescents progress towards maturity their approach to design tends to vary in a relatively characteristic manner. The differences found in their design work at various stages of their development are clearly reflected in their picture-making. A statement of this part of their work will be found in the following chapter in which further reference to design will be made. At the present, therefore, only a few general remarks about the attitudes of young people toward design need be made.

Children are intuitive designers and often produce work of great charm. The young adolescent, on the other hand, tends to be more concerned with the literary statement he wishes to make in his work, or in drawing in a manner which approaches photographic realism, than he is with an appropriate composition. His attention to realistic or literary statement causes his design to deteriorate from the standards to be found in the work of younger children. Later when his intellect is brought to bear upon design problems the standard of his work improves.

As was noted in the first chapter, one of the characteristics of adolescence is the marked development of the power to think. Changes in the nature and organization of mental ability occur with increasing age so that where conditions for learning are favourable, a pupil may continue to make intellectual gains of the type noted almost until the termination of his adolescence. These intellectual gains affect his work in design. As the pupil advances into adolescence he develops tendencies to consider problems of design from a more intellectual standpoint than was previously the case. This statement in no way infers that his emotions cease to function in a consideration of design. The emotions and the intellect never operate separately in any kind of behaviour, but rather appear in different intensities in varied situations. To a greater or lesser extent depending upon circumstances, an emotional aspect is always present when design is being approached. As well as including some emotional content, the maturing pupil, however, tends increasingly to employ his expanding intellectual abilities in solving problems of design.

12 "Seeing my Baby Sister for the First Time"—a painting in tempera by a 12-year-old girl. This pupil designs intuitively. Her interests still cling to the family.

3. Opposing Methods of Teaching Design

It was observed that in our schools today there exist two opposing methods of teaching design, and each is of long standing. In using the first method, the teacher decides upon a number of principles which he subsequently presents to the class as facts to be learned. Usually each fact is accompanied by a number of illustrations to prove each point. Later the pupils make their own designs to illustrate what they have learned, and perhaps to prove to the teacher that the various principles enunciated have been understood.

Although such an *a priori* method may appear to save time in a classroom, it has been the subject of some criticism. To start a student with superimposed order in design tends to prevent him from achieving an order of his own. Design is both a deep and a broad subject requiring much first-hand acquaintance with the various elements before any principle may be understood. It is questionable whether this method, as such, can ever lead to real insight into design, let alone to a personal feeling for it. Whatever responses the pupils develop to lessons presented according to this method seem to be simply quasi-intellectual verbalizations of an experience only partly understood.

A second method demands long experimentation on the part of the learners. In this method the teacher sets the stage for learning by arranging numerous activities (to be described presently[1]) involving the use of the elements of design. While each activity results in a design which is complete in itself, many of the activities may throw emphasis upon one or more of the elements. The possibilities with regard both to general learning and to the manipulation of materials inherent in this method are endless. Each activity must be suggested for the main purpose of helping the pupils to gain insight into the elements of design and their relationships to each other. Other pedagogical purposes occur, among which are included the development of taste, the improvement of skill connected with tools, processes, and techniques, the stimulation of initiative and the study of the possibilities and limitations of materials. Eventually it is to be expected that each pupil will arrive at

[1] *Seq.*, pp. 52-68.

some codification of his own regarding certain principles of design into which he has gained an insight by means of his own efforts.

4. Pragmatic Approach to the Principles of Design

It may be desirable in some respects to arrive at general principles of design, but if learning the list of principles is taken as the goal of the study, the result is unfortunate. The search for excellence of design must be continuous since perfection in art can never be reached completely. The most noticeable attitude prevalent when an art activity is engaging the attention of any reputable person is one in which the producer cannot rest in his search for improvement. Should the producer feel that he has reached a point of adequacy in his output, the quality of his work almost invariably suffers from then on. Art is the result of continuous effort to find a goal which is beyond one's present ability to reach. Its vitality is derived from this ever-present search for excellence. Throughout the history of man's artistic achievements one may find many examples of this statement. Paul Cézanne never ceased his explorations into the unknown and his work pulses with vitality. Jacques-Louis David adopted a codified aesthetic which he found in Classicism and for the most part his output is sterile and mechanical. In general, those artists of promise, who before their career has ended have come to rely upon formulae for their production, have invariably become stultified; those who have continued to seek for something better have maintained their role as creators of significant aesthetic forms.

A codification of principles can never be considered static, but rather, hypothetical. To be stimulating and not inhibiting, the principles of design can scarcely be considered in any but a pragmatic light in which they are held to be true only as long as they are effective for the person making a design. Because the scope of their intellect is expanding, this approach appears to be particularly attractive to young people. The adolescent finds it necessary constantly to review and revise his thinking about design. If at one stage of his studies he feels compelled to accept the orthodoxy of Classicism, his subsequent acquaintance with Impressionism will almost invariably cause him to modify his beliefs. A generalization formulated today may tomorrow be inadequate owing to new insights acquired through experience. In this method the maturing student appears to find a challenge and an aesthetic freedom, both of which he accepts gladly.

5. Ideas Requiring Generalization

It was found that the generalizations related to design eventually reached by students may be predicted in terms of whatever agreement has previously occurred in general aesthetics. With some help from the teacher, the pupil who is sufficiently mature intellectually, may be expected to reach some conclusions concerning the nature of unity in visual composition. Whenever design is considered thoughtfully the problem of achieving unity at once thrusts itself upon the creating person. However, the meaning of this concept will vary from person to person depending upon mental maturity, sensitivity and experience. In his consideration of unity of design in which he attempts to produce visual coherence in his composition, the student will be faced with such tasks as the development of a centre or centres of interest, the maintenance of balances and the arrangement of rhythms. (See Plates **20** and **22**.) He will learn through experience that a centre of interest may be formed through certain arrangements of any of the elements. Lines may lead to his chosen centre; contrasting textures, lights and darks, colours, masses and spaces may bring about desired effects. Rhythms may be developed in terms of the same elements and will be made apparent by means of a repetition of elements such as masses, colours and textures, or because of a flow of line. The many subtleties of balance will be felt and understood through experience with the elements. The thrusting line, the contrasting colour, the varied textures, the dark and light areas will each call for the attention of the observer and thus develop their own weight within the design. (See Plate **32**.)

As well as concerning himself with the problems leading to unity of design, a pupil must also consider the matter of variety. The chequer-board within its frame has a considerable unity but because of its lack of variety it has no signifi-

13 Examples of pottery by pupils in middle adolescence, showing an honest treatment of materials. The objects are designed in relation to their function.

cance as an art form. As in establishing unity of composition, so also in finding suitable variety, the student must perform many experiments and enjoy many experiences with the elements of design before he can develop feeling and understanding in this aspect of composition. (See Plates **14** and **17**.)

Other matters related to composition including an honest treatment of the materials employed and the production of an adequate design in relation to its function must constantly confront the pupil. (See Plates **19** and **23**.) He must be encouraged to use materials with sensitivity so that their inherent qualities are employed to the best advantage. He should learn that an intelligent use of material, or a combination of materials, greatly enhances a design. He will discover through experience that the ways in which most materials may be used are almost limitless. He will learn, for example, that although oil paint has been employed by artists for many centuries, experiments such as those performed by Braque continue to be made with this medium, and new techniques discovered. By using some of the newer media, such as the commercially prepared casein paints and the new lacquers and by combining established media, his scope for exploration is vast. (See Plate 38.) In materials themselves the student may find an ever-present challenge again demanding an attitude of open-mindedness and a willingness to experiment.

It is safe to say that the best designs for most objects have probably not yet been invented. The pupil will realize that a few simple objects such as the axe, have at the present time come as close to perfection as human beings can make them. Nevertheless, even the design of such a basic object as the axe might be altered should superior materials which might be used in this tool be discovered. Good designers are continually seeking better designs, not only for relatively new objects such as automobiles and aeroplanes, but also for those objects which man has been making for centuries, such as hoes, chairs, fireplaces and of course paintings. To find the design which best suits its purpose presents another exciting challenge for the student.

Because in all these matters concerning design the ultimate has not yet been reached, the road lies open for any student to discover something new. The only sure principle of design for him is that beyond his present aesthetic horizon lies a better design than that which he has just produced. Only by maintaining this dynamic attitude can he find some personal mastery of art. The teacher of art has the duty of encouraging adolescents to maintain this attitude whenever a problem of design is being considered.

6. Activities Placing Emphasis Upon Specific Elements of Design

As mentioned previously, to produce a design is to perform a complete aesthetic act. There is in reality no justification for the term "applied design", because the design itself is an integral part of all art output. To paraphrase an analogy used by the late Benedetto Croce, the intellectual dissection of a work

DESIGN EXPERIENCES FOR ADOLESCENTS 53

14 Making a piece of mobile sculpture. This pupil is experimenting with the elements and principles of design by producing a complete art form.

of art into its elements arrives at the same results as a dissection of a human body into nerves, organs and the like; in both cases we are left with a corpse. It is always a dangerous practice to attempt to disintegrate a subject for administrative or teaching purposes. Nevertheless, in order to assist a learner more conveniently to sift through an otherwise confusing body of experience with design in general, the teacher may arrange certain situations in the art room which will give direction and point to design activities. Such arrangements concern the elements of design.

Writers of aesthetics have made many attempts to define the elements of design. Agreement has been reached in a definition of a number of such elements and a standard vocabulary, to some degree at least, has been formulated. That some disagreement exists in the matter of the elements is to be expected since the subject is a philosophical one. Moreover, the subject of design is doubly difficult to explain in words since it includes experiences which must be felt in such a way as to defy adequate verbalization. The elements upon which there

15 Weaving on a floor loom. No matter what type of art activity engages a pupil, a problem in design is automatically involved.

in some agreement are as follows: line; mass and space; light and shade; texture; colour. Volume is often spoken of as an extension of mass and space. Writers have defined several other elements but on these there is less unanimity of opinion.

It is with the elements over which there is considerable agreement that a student must have many of his experiences. A purely intellectual or verbal study of them would be quite inadequate. While a number of facts about them might be learned and could be enunciated parrot fashion, a deep, meaningful and organic insight into design comes only from the struggle to create art forms.

Some examples of design activities which, while resulting in the production of satisfying art forms, throw emphasis upon specific elements are suggested below. Each of the activities mentioned has been tested in all grades from seven to twelve. Broadly speaking, it was found that the activities begin to be effective as means of assisting pupils to gain greater insight into design only in the ninth grade or when the pupils are approaching middle adolescence. For younger pupils, who as a rule have not yet consciously developed problems in design and hence who feel little need of formal instruction in this work, the activities did not appear to be particularly useful.

Pupils in early adolescence can be helped to improve the design which is found in their picture-making and other expressive work of a similar kind. The young pupil will often profit from guidance in design if it is closely linked with his general art activities, because by means of such assistance he learns to be more successful in those artistic acts which he understands and enjoys. By helping these pupils in this incidental manner, the teacher is paving the way for more formal studies in design. The discussions which evolve from the teacher's remarks should have the purpose of assisting the pupils both to define their problems in more abstract terms and to develop a basic vocabulary in this field of thought. The development of a precise vocabulary is most important if effective thought is eventually to be given to design, and a beginning in vocabulary building should be made early in adolescence. Later when the pupils' abilities to think about design in abstract terms are more advanced, they may approach the subject in a more formal manner, and with a vocabulary sufficiently broad to meet their requirements.

Pupils from the ninth to the twelfth grade demonstrated in most cases a considerable interest in formal design activities and were able eventually to achieve commendable results in them. The results depended upon the skill, insight and maturity possessed by each pupil, so that the older pupils tended to have the greatest success in this work.

Line.

This element is perhaps the most revealing of personality and as such, lends itself most readily to expressive work in art. Likewise, it reveals in the most obvious manner competence in the matter of skill and sensitivity. Perhaps the simplest activity in this connection is found in the production of a non-objective line drawing. Sometimes stimulus may come from music and practice may at first be had by moving the hands rhythmically without making marks with the chalk, conté crayon, or whatever medium may be chosen for the work. A study of nature in movement including the waves of the sea, the tossing of branches, or the motion of clouds or smoke may also be represented with rhythmic lines. Effective work in line of a more demanding nature may also be found in "contour drawing" of which Picasso is a master. Here the pupil draws only in outline the contours of life or still-life objects. (See Plate 8.)

It might be noted in this and other activities involving subjects taken from life and still-life that a sensitive use of line, rather than a photographic representation of the objects seen, should be encouraged. Since the aesthetic vision of pupils varies they should be allowed to approach the subject according to their own inclinations, establishing as they work their own techniques of thinking, as well as of drawing. While the persons who rely upon a visual image for expressive purposes may keep their eyes continually on an object while drawing, those who are more inclined to express the thoughts generated by the things they observe may not wish to refer to the stimulus of their expression once drawing has begun.

The element of line includes the measured line as well as that which is free-flowing. In considering the properties of the measured line the pupil may experiment with geometrical designs which involve mathematical arrangements. (See Plates **16**, **18**, and **23**.) Paper sculpture lends itself readily to geometric work. (See Plate **35**.) An interesting study will be found in resolving certain natural forms into geometric patterns. As an example of this type of work one might cite the seashell or nautilus which the Greeks resolved into the volute of the capital of the Ionian order of architectural column.

During his study of line, the adolescent should have brought to his attention the output of others in which this element has been used effectively. Reproductions or originals of such work as Rembrandt's etchings or Henry Moore's sketches are types of professional work which might inspire young people at this time. The pupils might be expected occasionally to

16 Three-dimensional geometric design. This disciplined art form involving a measured line was made from thin strips of wood. To add variety to his work, the pupil has painted some strips black and some white, and has covered two areas with black paper.

17 A study of space and tones of grey, with one colour added. In this formal study particular attention has been paid to space relationships.

make a line analysis of some professional work being studied. The study of professional work in relation to the art activity in progress is to be encouraged no matter what may be the subject under consideration.

Mass and Space.

The elements of mass and space refer to the shape and proportions of the objects placed in a composition, as well as to the spaces which surround them. (See Plate **19**.) Mass may almost automatically thrust itself upon the attention of a pupil although his taste in the matter of resolving an object into an aesthetic mass must be developed by means of practice. He sometimes tends to forget the element of space as having equal importance in relation to a composition. Since mass cannot logically exist apart from space both the elements must be considered together. A dot placed anywhere upon an otherwise blank page, for example, immediately brings both elements into play.

One effective activity involving mass and space may be found in making a montage from grey or brown paper of no pronounced texture. Various shapes are cut from the paper and are later moved over a surface of contrasting tone until a satisfactory arrangement is discovered. Non-objective paintings in the manner of Mondrian may be produced also, in which space division is emphasized. (See Plate 17.)

What may be called a "point and line" design, which presents problems related to space division and to the arrangement of masses is an effective activity. Pins with large heads are stuck into a board and are connected with thread. By moving the positions of some of the pins or by adding others, infinite possibilities for space division may be found. (See Plate 18.)

Life and still-life studies may be made in which the masses of the objects are emphasized by means of drawing lines from contour to contour, in the manner of Henry Moore, so that the spaces are carefully designed between the masses.

Many actual three-dimensional activities may place emphasis upon mass and space. Mobile sculpture comes first to mind in providing problems of space relationships as well as of aesthetic and physical balance. (See Plate 14.) Pupils should have drawn to their attention in this connection the output of Calder. Non-objective sculpture in any of a variety of materials such as paper, wood and plaster of paris, are also valuable in this study. (See Plate 34.) The making of families of sculptured pieces, in which a satisfying mass and space relationship must be achieved not only within each individual piece, but also when two or three such pieces are brought into close spacial proximity with one another adds some fascinating problems. (See Plate 19.) A further activity involving the elements in question may be found in making designs with thin strips of wood with the approximate thickness of a toothpick. Medical sticks for swabs may be used here, and geometrical designs or free forms may be devised in which certain areas may be covered with paper to provide variety. (See Plate 16.) Similar designs may also be made with string attached to the five areas of an open box.

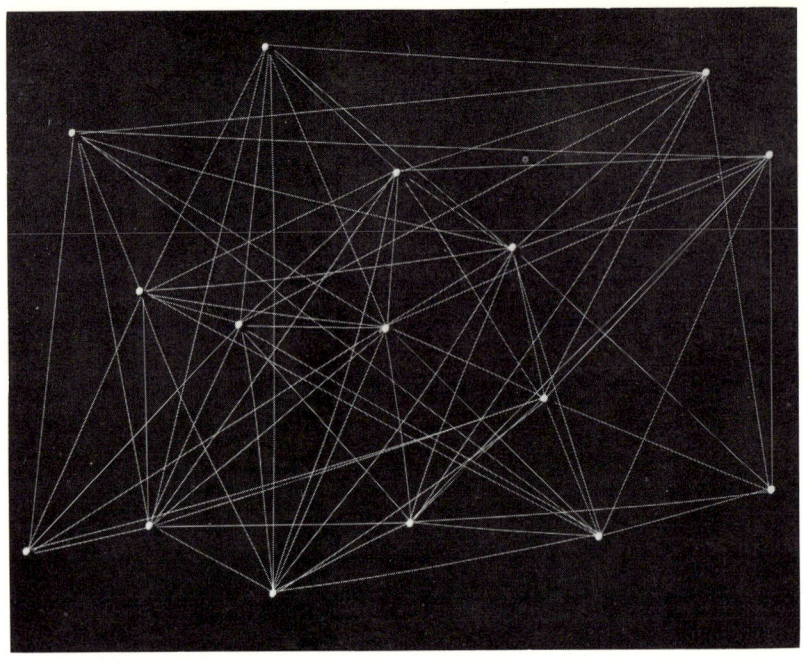

18 A "point and line" design. White-headed pins and white cotton thread were carefully arranged on a dark background to arrive at a striking relationship of geometrical areas.

Light and Shade.

    Many of the activities previously noted, when given a slightly different emphasis may draw attention to the elements of light and shade. Life and still-life work may now be rendered in dark and light areas. Non-objective patterns in tones of grey may be made. (See Plate **17**.) Non-objective sculpture may be devised in terms of high-lights and shadows upon itself and with respect to the shadows it casts upon various surfaces. (See Plate **19**.) Increased emphasis upon light and shade may be devised by placing the objects being designed in the path of a strong beam of light. Strong shadows cast upon a wall as the result of placing a piece of mobile sculpture in a spotlight will illustrate the importance of light and shade as significant elements of design, while shadows thrown from one piece of sculpture to another will do the same. Interesting effects may be arranged by beaming one or more sources of light into a small

19 Non-objective sculpture in plaster of paris. This illustrates a problem in design in which three objects are made, each different from the others, but all having a "family" resemblance. Here one finds a study of variety in unity.

enclosed space like a miniature stage, and subsequently blocking some of the light with carefully formed non-objective shapes. This type of controlled blocking of light may also be used upon a semi-transparent textile screen such as silk, in the manner of a shadow-puppet production.

Texture.

Students should have experiences with textures of two kinds; those which are actual and those which are drawn or painted. In a woven textile one may find actual rough and smooth places according to the warp and weft threads used. In a drawing or painting, a series of dots of colour or some cross-hatched lines may appear to be rough in comparison with a wash of colour. Each type of texture carries with it its own aesthetic impact. Among many others, John Piper and

Yasuo Kuniyoshi are both worth studying for the textural effects which may be achieved in painting.

Some of the importance of textural effects may be learned by working textures upon a plain and malleable surface such as a sheet of silver foil. Non-objective arrangements using scraps of textile glued to a support of cardboard or wood, or non-objective drawings in pen and ink in which many methods may be found to produce the effect of various textures, may also be tried. Oil paint to which extra substances such as sand and sawdust are added may be employed. Interesting textural effects may be derived from a montage in which clippings of printed material found in newspapers and magazines are brought together into non-objective relationships. Loom-weaving provides one of the most efficient activities to teach textures.

Colour.

Colour has often been described as the most important of the elements for the reason that it has the strongest emotional impact. In comparatively recent years some writers have tended to minimize this assertion on the grounds that the other elements have an equally important, if n*ot* greater impact in aesthetic composition and are more closely linked to the nature of our physical existence. Whatever the truth may be of the relative importance of colour as an element of design, the fact remains that colour has been the subject of an extraordinary amount of research. Not only Chevreul, Helmholtz and Ostwold, who were concerned primarily with scientific matters, but also artists of ability such as Seurat and Signac have contributed to the systematization of colour theory. Largely as a result of their research, several systems for the use of colour have evolved and have often been offered to pupils as a short-cut to learning how to use the elements. It must be pointed out that in order to use colour effectively, it must be used personally and that, as in the case of the other elements, a sensitive use of colour can result only after prolonged experience with it. This statement does not rule out the use of colour charts or wheels while the student is learning about hue, chroma and intensity, but the statement does deny the validity

20 Montage with cut paper and coloured inks. Careful planning has gone into this arrangement by an 18-year-old pupil. The work is imaginative and approaches structural coherence.

of teaching formalized arrangements or colour schemes devised by others. The unfortunate results in design which occur when a person is largely governed by an intellectual theory in the use of colour are clearly, if unintentionally, demonstrated by Birren in the illustrations to be found in his *Monument to Colour*. There are no irrefutable aesthetic laws concerning the use of colour, nor has any one pigment in and by itself any

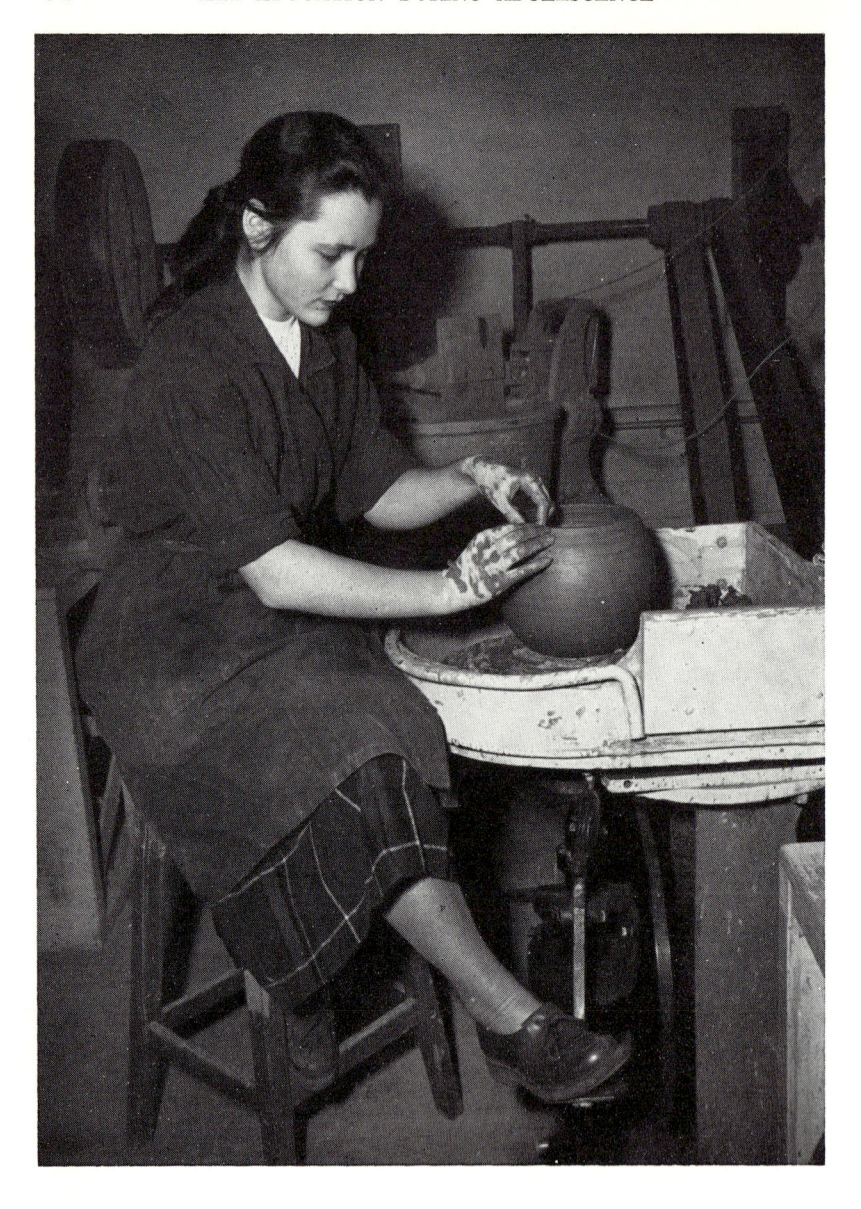

21 Working at the potter's wheel. Unless the basic form of the object is right it will be a failure as art, no matter what colours are later applied in the glazes.

special inherent property such as hot or cold, distant or near. Only when related to another colour or colours does it take to itself special significance. The "hottest" red paint on the end of a painter's brush loses its "heat" next to a geranium in the sun or to a tube of neon gas vibrating in red-wave lengths. Placed next to blue or grey pigment it may then grow warm or advance. Before a teacher is tempted to offer pupils formulae for the use of colour, he might reflect that after hundreds of years of experience on the part of artists, contemporary painters cannot yet entirely agree upon even the so-called primary colours.

Experience with colour may be introduced so readily in the classroom that methods need scarcely be mentioned. Colour may be introduced in any of the activities mentioned in connection with the foregoing discussion of the elements. Indeed, colour must always be associated with one or more of the other elements; a dot of pigment on a canvas, for example, immediately involves mass and space as well as colour. Non-objective arrangements may be made in which colour takes its rightful place, but before such compositions can be devised, other elements must be carefully arranged. (See Plates **17** and **20**.) Unless consideration is given to other elements the arrangement produced would be a chaos of colour and not a design structure at all. In spite of this, colour is a powerful element and its careless handling may easily disintegrate an otherwise coherent aesthetic organization. The teacher must be ready to assist learners to arrive at means of developing appropriate tones in a composition, for upon tone lies significance in the use of colour. Of tremendous assistance to pupils is the study of the work of many of the great colourists including such geniuses as El Greco, Tintoretto, Turner, Renoir, Van Gogh and Gauguin. One may conclude that colour may be most effectively studied only in connection with a complete problem of design in which the majority of the other elements are brought into play. (See Plates **23**, **32**, **33**, **36** and **38**.)

7. Summary

Design is an integral part of any artistic expression and therefore cannot be considered as a separate and distinct form

22 Non-objective design in tempera by a pupil in middle adolescence. He has arranged subtle variations of masses and spaces in his composition, but has become over-exuberant in his use of textural effects. Such faults occur not infrequently during this period of development, but tend to disappear in later adolescence if suitable guidance is provided.

DESIGN EXPERIENCES FOR ADOLESCENTS 67

of art activity. Adolescents follow a relatively characteristic pattern of behaviour in treating design problems. In early adolescence they tend to neglect design in the interest of realistic statements, but with approaching maturity comes an interest in this work often of an intellectual nature. Design should be taught in a manner which allows great freedom of thought and action on the part of the producer and which is consistent with his ability to use his intellect. A formal study of design is usually not effective until a pupil reaches the ninth grade or middle adolescence. Formulae for the principles of design should never be given. A pupil may be helped to master

23 Three-dimensional organization in coloured plastics. This design problem placed emphasis upon the measured line, the relationships between masses and spaces and upon colour effects when transparent materials are used.

problems of design by developing an adequate vocabulary and by performing many activities, each of which places particular emphasis upon one or two of the elements only. Complete separation of the elements cannot occur and this is especially noticeable in the case of colour.

ADDITIONAL READING:

Clive Bell. *Art*. New York: F. A. Stokes Co., 1920.

Faber Birren. *Monument to Colour*. New York: McFarlane Warde McFarlane, 1938.

N. I. Cannon. *Pattern and Design*. London: Lund Humphries, 1948.

John Dewey. *Art as Experience*. New York: Minton, Balch & Co., 1934.

Roger Fry. *Vision and Design*. London: Chalto & Windus, 1920.

Gyorgi Kepes. *Language of Vision*. Chicago: Paul Theobald, 1944.

Bernard Leach. *A Potter's Portfolio: A Selection of Fine Pots*. London: Lund Humphries and Company Limited, 1951.

Laszlo Maholy-Nagy. *The New Vision*. New York: W. W. Norton and Co. Inc., 1938.

Ralph L. Wickeser. *An Introduction to Art Activities*. New York: Henry Holt & Co., 1947.

Chapter VI

PICTURE-MAKING BY ADOLESCENTS

1. The Nature of Picture-Making

As has been stated previously, any divisions set up within the framework of art activities are likely to be arbitrary. What the differences may be between picture-making and design-making, no one in the last analysis may tell. In this chapter, picture-making refers to those two-dimensional activities in which pupils present a record of their reactions to life experiences in terms of a drawing or a painting employing all the necessary elements of design.

As shown in Chapter I, a study of adolescents quickly reveals that there is no standard type of adolescent personality. Each person is the product of his peculiar biological inheritance and of his environmental conditions. Since production in art is a revelation of personality, one might deduce that the pictures produced by pupils are as varied as the personalities of their authors. Young children have not been subjected to environmental conditions for as long as have adolescents. Consequently, if one may judge from their overt acts, they have not developed such marked divergencies of personality as the older pupils and they tend to produce pictures exhibiting fairly obviously a more or less regular pattern of development. Such is not the case with adolescents and any pattern of development which may exist in their pictorial output is more difficult to detect.

Of all art forms, pictures are usually the most revealing of personality and hence of personal developmental patterns. Pictures tend to reveal a pupil's emotional and intellectual reactions to environment, his insights into the nature of artistic endeavour in general and his sensitivity with regard to design more clearly than any other type of art production. For these reasons a large number of pictures were selected for the kind of analysis found in this chapter.

2. Some Trends in Adolescent Picture-Making

Any investigation designed to gain insight into trends in the output of pictures by adolescents must be based first, upon many cases and second, upon cases influenced by widely differing environments. In order to meet these requirements, nearly 6,000 pictures were studied in one way or another. These pictures were produced by pupils enrolled in grades seven to twelve, in 240 schools in all regions of the Province of Ontario. That is to say, the schools were selected in large cities, in suburban areas and in rural sections. Some of the schools enrolled pupils from industrial parts of cities, and some from residential sections. The schools were situated in widely differing geographical areas; from the heavily populated south—with its comparatively mild climate and settled ways of life, to the sparsely populated north where a pioneer spirit is to be found and where the climatic conditions tend to be rigorous.

As shown in Chapter III no known scale exists in which a picture or any other art form may be graded accurately. Any appraisal of pictures is open to question on the grounds concerning the necessarily subjective techniques which must be employed. Nevertheless, in order to gain some insight into the degree of success in picture-making achieved by adolescents found in the various grade levels, a technique of research was chosen which at the present time appears to be the most valid available and the one which is used almost universally in professional artistic circles. A jury composed of qualified people interested in art and art education was asked to pass opinions concerning each of the pictures submitted from the 240 schools, and was requested to state to what extent it believed the pupils had been successful in producing pieces of art. The members of the jury, in other words, were asked to appraise the pictures according to their significance as artistic records of reactions to life experiences. Thus design in relation to subject matter, originality of vision on the part of the producer, facility with the media employed, and like attributes of good production in art were brought under observation. Criteria for success were those commonly used by any art jury and thus the work was considered from an art standpoint and not as the by-product of an educational process. The

PICTURE-MAKING BY ADOLESCENTS 71

24 "Glenna's Wedding"—a painting in tempera by a 12-year-old girl. She depicts her interests in romantic and social affairs. Her technical abilities are sufficiently developed to satisfy her present requirements in pictorial expression. Some of the naïve charm of childlike art clings to her work.

work observed was not to be graded in any manner, but accepted or rejected entirely on the basis as to whether it was art or not.

According to findings derived from these procedures, the degree of success which adolescent pupils achieve varies as one might expect, from grade to grade. A uniform increase from one grade to the next was not found, however. Starting with the seventh grade, the jury found that about 10 percent of the pictures could be considered successful. Of the eighth grade work, slightly less than five percent of the pictures were said to fall into this category. The lowest point was not reached, however, until the ninth grade where only about three percent of the pictures were found to be successful. Between the ninth and tenth grades, a sharp improvement began to be noted so that 11 percent of the pictures were selected. Improvement continued throughout the following two grades. In the eleventh grade, 19 percent of the pictures were found to be successful and the rise continued throughout the twelfth grade, but not quite as sharply as in the three previous grades. In the twelfth grade about 23 percent of the pictures were placed in the "success" category. The following table gives a graphic picture of the findings.

TABLE I—PERCENTAGES BY GRADES OF PICTURES CONSIDERED TO BE SUCCESSFUL

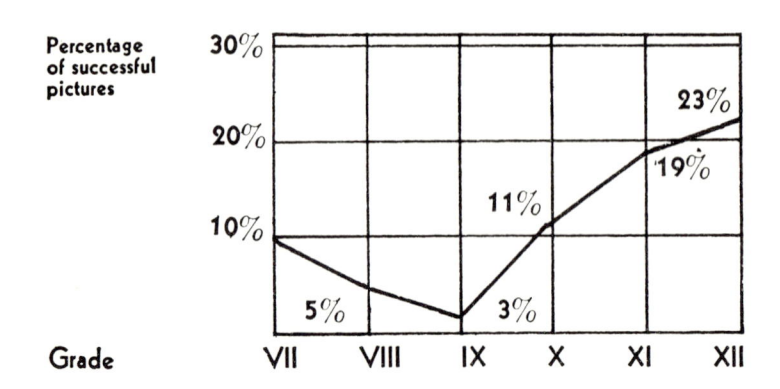

Grade	VII	VIII	IX	X	XI	XII
Percentage of successful pictures	10%	5%	3%	11%	19%	23%

25 "The Accident"—a painting in tempera. The 13-year-old painter is more concerned with factual representation than he is with problems of pictorial composition.

From the findings it appears that with the onset of adolescence, pupils find rapidly increasing difficulty with pictorial expression and that in the ninth grade, they experience the greatest difficulties. In reading the graph, however, one must take into account the fact that the pupils in the eleventh and twelfth are more highly selected, because of the tendency to drop out of school between grades nine and ten as revealed in the enrolment charts of the provincial school system. Also since many pupils transfer from one school to another at the end of the eighth grade they may be unsettled in their new situation. Nevertheless, even taking into account adverse conditions related to enrolment and placement, there appears to be an indication that the early stage of adolescence mentioned in Chapter I through which the pupil usually passes while enrolled in the seventh to the ninth grades, tends to interfere with his output in picture-making.

26 "Slum Clearance"—a drawing in tempera by a 12-year-old boy. He demonstrates an interest in technique and has experimented in this work with stick-painting.

3. Some Experiments Related to the Continuity of the Picture-Making Programme

The findings of the jury gave rise to several problems. First, should picture-making be eliminated from the programme of studies in art for those pupils experiencing difficulty with his activity? Second, if picture-making should be eliminated, for how long? Third, since findings related to picture-making must be indicative of those related to any branch of art, should art be eliminated entirely from the school programme during the early stages of adolescence?

In an attempt to answer these questions some experiments were conducted. One group of 115 pupils who had studied art from the first grade up to the eighth grade, was not allowed to make pictures in grade nine. A second group of 87 pupils who had studied art as far as the end of the seventh grade, was not allowed any picture-making activities during the eighth and ninth grades. Both groups were allowed some optional art activities including ceramics, weaving, and puppetry exclusive of the painting of back-drops and other pictorial work. A third group of 246 pupils who likewise had studied art up to the end of the seventh year, was offered no art activities whatsoever in the eighth and ninth grades. All three groups resumed a study of art, with special emphasis upon picture-making, in the tenth grade.

The pictures produced in the tenth grade by all three groups were appraised by the jury composed of most of the same people who performed the judging mentioned previously. The same criteria used in judging the first group of pictures were again employed. In the opinion of the members of the jury the lowest standard of production in picture-making was found in the group which had been offered no art activities whatsoever. The group which had been offered alternative studies in art for two years also produced pictures of a low, but slightly higher standard than the group having no art activities at all. The group which had been offered alternative studies for one year produced pictures of a somewhat higher standard than the pupils employed for two years with alternative studies. None of the groups, in the opinion of the jury, reached a standard comparable with that of pupils who were able to experience picture-making without interruption. Furthermore, observation of some pupils in each of three groups deprived of picture-making seemed to indicate a deterioration of interest in the making of pictures.

Of the total number of pupils, namely 448, in the three groups studied, 36 continued a study of picture-making in the eleventh grade. Of these, only 6 appeared to reach a standard of picture-making equal to that of their classmates who had enjoyed uninterrupted experience in this work.

One may conclude from these experiments first, that an interruption in the picture-making programme of adolescents, even during the years in which they appear to find most difficulty with this work, adversely affects the standard of their production in this field when they resume work in it. Second, the longer the interruption, the lower appears to be the standard of work once the activity is resumed. Third, the majority of pupils whose picture-making programme is interrupted for a length of time ranging from one to two years produce work of a lower standard than pupils whose pro-

27 "Window Cleaning"—a painting in tempera. The 13-year-old painter is in a transition stage in which a "realistic" approach is beginning to be modified by aesthetic considerations.

gramme is not curtailed, and the adverse effects of this interruption are noticeable for at least two years after the picture-making programme is resumed. Fifth, to substitute other art activities in the place of picture-making seems not to compensate fully for the lost experience in this activity. It would appear that pupils should if possible, enjoy a continuous programme of picture-making throughout their entire adolescence if they wish to achieve a maximum degree of success in it during later adolescence.

The fact that a panel of experts found a relatively low percentage of success in picture-making during early adolescence, evidently does not take into account the benefits derived from art education in general by those who were not apparently successful in their endeavours. Learning of a broad nature which is claimed to accompany art education and which includes an improvement of taste, a deeper understanding and appreciation of the environment, a greater appreciation for the creative efforts of others, a development of initiative, and perhaps most important of all, an increased emotional stability probably occur as a result of work in art during early adolescence no matter what the actual standard of the art output at this time may be. That such additional learnings do take place during early adolescence is suggested by the fact that a steady improvement occurs in picture-making once the personal difficulties of the pupil are resolved.

Also of major importance in the data recorded is the indication that art education should continue into the higher levels of secondary education, for it is only here that its effects reach any kind of fruition. To curtail art education at the end of the eighth or ninth grade, a common practice today in general education, is to close off at a critical stage a major field of human endeavour in which a strong educational force is operative. The benefits of art education with its gratifying effects upon the maturing individual can evidently be realized to their full extent only by maintaining this study until the pupil has progressed into the later stages of adolescence. In spite of academic pressures, it would appear that art education in the secondary schools should receive much more encouragement than is the case at present. Any adolescent with his need

28 "Spring Cleaning"—a painting in tempera by a 16-year-old boy. This painter in middle adolescence is concerned with detail, although he pays considerable attention to pictorial composition. His ability to draw is rapidly improving.

for emotional outlets, his sensitivity and his latent creative abilities, is in a position to profit considerably from what art education has to offer.

4. Some Characteristics of Picture-Making by Adolescents at Various Stages of Development

For the purpose of learning about the effects of maturation upon the behaviour and output of pupils engaged in art activities, a number of observations were made. Some 200 boys and girls between ten and eighteen years of age were selected for careful observation. As many as possible of the pupils continued to be studied at regular intervals for nearly six years, while their art work was filed. By this means, the pupils were observed throughout all stages of adolescent development and samples of their pictures produced during each stage were preserved. Later, additional pictures, the work of pupils submitted from schools in the Province at large were added to the collection for subsequent examination. The conclusions reached as a result of this study follow.

(i) *Pre-adolescent output in art compared generally with that of adolescents.*

The pre-adolescent approaches expression almost wholly intuitively. He is confident of his powers, puts his ideas quickly and easily into pictorial form and is satisfied with his results. He tends to be egocentric in his selection of subject matter. He is not ready to accept much criticism from his teacher nor can he offer much self-criticism. His skill is restricted by his muscular development, just as his ideas are limited by his intellectual powers. During the early years of adolescence the pupil appears to lose much of this self-confidence in his ability to produce pictures. With his growing intellectual powers he appears to become self-critical to a degree which interferes with such organized and disciplined acts of expression as picture-making. Not until middle adolescence, at which time he gains greater control of his motor and intellectual abilities and of his emotional reactions, does he begin to find increased success in his picture-making activities. Beginning in middle adolescence and often extending into a later period, he reaches a degree of success comparable

29 "Sketch in the Classroom"—a wash drawing in which water-colour was used. The 15-year-old pupil shows interest in life drawing and is concerned with pictorial composition.

with that achieved during the pre-adolescent stage. Although the degrees of success may be comparable, the forms of expression and the patterns of behaviour found in full adolescence as opposed to pre-adolescence vary considerably in several important respects.

(ii) *Early Adolescence (about Grades VII to IX inclusive)*.

In early adolescence the pupil's interests appear sometimes to be still rather closely tied to the family. (See Plate **12**.) His subjects may depict family affairs in which he participates as an equal among group-ups:

> Starting the furnace when Mother and Dad were away.
> Using the new washing machine.
> Building our rock garden.

He shows interest also in many novel, unique or daring experiences:

> Taking the "Devil's Elbow" on skis.
> A fight in a hockey game.
> The bank hold-up.
> Climbing the television tower.

Closely allied to these topics are those in which he selects as subject matter sporting events which include members of his social group. Games in which he can excel individually may be used as subject matter. Any topic of a physically challenging or generally strenuous nature may be selected.

Themes which present a challenge to the imagination also are popular. Such themes may derive from films, reading, television, or from some other vicarious source.

>The space ship to Mars.
>The war of the worlds.
>We conquer Mount Everest.
>The capture of Quebec.

Portraiture and life studies arouse occasional interest in this age group although life drawing as an activity in its own right does not seem to have marked appeal. Human figures in pictures are sometimes drawn with anatomical details of a rather pronounced nature. This appears to indicate a growing interest in some of the visible sex characteristics of the maturing body. Little interest on the other hand is shown in still-life work.

Certain activities which to an adult are commonplace but which to a young person are admired because they are considered part of the world of men and women, may frequently be selected as themes for picture-making. In this classification of subjects, the sex of the pupil has perhaps the greatest bearing upon the choice of theme.

>Buying a pair of skates.
>Going to the hairdresser.
>Driving the car.
>Getting ready for the dance.

Subject matter of this type sometimes degenerates into banality since it fails to be relieved either by a design which might be considered competent or by the fresh and naïve design of a child. The pupil's growing intellectual powers often lead him to seek extreme "realism" or a photographic accuracy in the delineation of objects making up his compositions. The search for realism of this sort frustrates him upon two counts; in the first place he lacks the skill to produce such work; in the second, this type of delineation usually interferes with an artistic result. These young people resort to another type of composition involving the photographic drawing of objects to illustrate themes which are little understood. In this class of work the objects are presented as symbols; a wine glass, a bottle marked XXX, a hand holding a long cigarette holder and a smoking cigarette might be placed on paper to illustrate the subject "High Society". Similar work with different symbols might be used for such subjects as "Jazz", "Murder" or "Rhythm". Since the objects used are commonplace and because they are usually jumbled together on the page without much thought to pictorial composition, the results are aesthetically repellent.

In most of the pictures examined, the designs employed by these young people were disappointing. Often it appeared normal for them to ignore design. Because the pictorial viewpoint was frequently too wide for successful composition, the space arrangements were without interest. Frequently the pupil would include say, large areas of land and sky, or of wall and floor, regardless of the message he wished to convey. Not only were the spaces without interest, but also the masses lacked the organization which an intelligent placement in space and an overlapping of objects might have achieved. Line was often used without regard for its flexibility and character and merely in the capacity of outline. More often than not it was broken, hesitant and without direction. Colour was sometimes used throughout the composition in standard hues leading to a chaos of brilliance. At other times, tempera paint or water colour was thinned so that it lost character and interest. Light and shade when used, frequently lacked subtlety and appeared in intense black or pure white with little gradation between high lights and shadows. Texture was usually not employed for aesthetic purposes, although it was used to portray a surface such as metal or fur.

Probably because he feels insecure the young person will resort to copying. At times he admires the technique of another person and allows it to influence him unduly. At other times he will try to copy some professional in every respect. This serves only to handicap him in attaining some personal mastery of art.

Pupils during this stage of development often display a clumsiness in using familiar tools and media. Their span of attention is inclined to be short, so that a forty-minute period of work often appears to exhaust their interest in the art activity engaging their attention.

Not all young people exhibit the tendencies described above and some of those who do so quickly progress to a more encouraging phase of development. Early adolescence, however, is, in general, potentially a difficult period for the teacher as well as the pupil.

While suitable guidance must be forthcoming at this time, the teacher must resist any temptation to hurry the pupils into more mature forms of behaviour before they are ready to take such a step. Likewise, perhaps the even greater temptation must be resisted of attempting to hold them to childish forms of expression in which they found success during pre-adolescence. This is a period demanding sympathetic and thoughtful guidance, tact and continued faith in youth. The characteristics of picture-making of the period are simply manifestations of the business of growing up.

(iii) *Middle Adolescence (about Grades VIII to Grade X inclusive)*.

The second period of adolescence usually is much more encouraging to both pupils and teachers. At this time the pupil achieves more success in his activities and he shows greater tendencies to profit from guidance.

In middle adolescence the pupil tends to omit in his picture-making subject matter having reference to the family. If the family receives comment, it may be in a rather humorous vein.

> My sister learns to drive a car.
> My father tries his hand as a carpenter.

Items of childhood experience may be occasionally unearthed from the memory and used as subject matter. (See Plate 12.)

> How I discovered there was no Santa Claus.
> When I first saw my baby sister.

The chief interest appears to lie in social activities involving particular friends, in acts of daring or in forbidden experience, in sports and in life at large where the pupil has partici-

30 "One Minute to Nine"—a painting in water-colour. A 17-year-old girl depicts in humourous vein an event at school. Although by no means of a professional standard, her draughtsmanship and pictorial arrangement are adequate.

pated as an adult. (See Plate **24**.) Vocational interests associated with summer employment receive notice (see Plate **27**) and such themes are often reminiscent of early adolescence. The drama of these occasions is at times very much overdrawn.

>At the dance.
>Going on a hike.
>The picnic.
>Experimenting in the chemistry lab.
>Driving in the stock car races.
>Running the tractor.
>Working for the Hydro-Electric Company
>   in my holidays.
>Fire in the apartment building.

Sometimes social themes are given serious attention. (See Plate **26**.)

>In the heart of the city.
>Slum clearance.
>Sidewalk playground.

Occasionally pupils, especially girls, manifest at this level an interest in a fanciful, idealistic world which they may depict with considerable sensitivity and a degree of thoughtful introspection. This subject matter is distinct from the "science fiction" topics of an earlier period:

>Reflection in the water.
>On first hearing Beethoven's
>   *Moonlight Sonata.*
>Castles in the clouds.
>Dream landscape.

Music selected by the teacher having a pronounced rhythmic beat or with a vivid pictorial content, together with selected literary themes provide inspiration:

>*Rhapsody in Blue* (Gershwin)
>*Masquerade* (Khachaturian)
>*Firebird* (Stravinsky)
>*Scheherazade* (Rimski-Korsakov)
>*Romeo and Juliet* (Shakespeare-Tchaikovsky)
>*Midsummer Night's Dream* (Shakespeare-
>   Mendelssohn)
>*Swan Lake* (Tchaikovsky)
>*Peter Grimes* (Britten)
>*The Consul* (Minotti)

Life, portraiture, still-life and landscape become increasingly popular as art forms in themselves, and not as a means of producing pictures which present in a literary manner events which occur in the lives of the pupils.

In middle adolescence the pupil's approach to picture-making is found to be one of transition. The intuitive approach to design seen almost universally in pre-adolescence and sometimes in early adolescence, gives away in many instances to one in which the intellect is brought increasingly into play. Some pupils, however, continue to produce work intuitively and often they are successful in so doing. Nevertheless, a tendency may be noted in which an intellectualization of design and of technique is apparent. As noted in the previous chapter, discussions pertaining to the possible relationships of the elements of design, with a subsequent manipulation of materials to gain desired effects, and also a study of the techniques of others are welcomed as art activities. It is during this period also that pupils begin to set standards for themselves which they may or may not possess sufficient skill to achieve. In an attempt to fathom something of the relationship of design and technique to picture-making, the pupil is sometimes given to extravagant experimentation. As one might expect, many experiments of this nature end in failure to produce a noteworthy art form. The experience derived from the manipulation of materials is valuable since the experimentation involved is conducted with definite purpose, and hence it results in considerable learning.

While searching for an adequate technique, the middle adolescent not infrequently becomes unduly influenced by that of either some well-known and perhaps fashionable professional painter or some particular school of painting. He may come under the spell of Piper, the Englishman; Shahn, the American; Milne, the Canadian; or Dufy, the Frenchman. He may be attracted to Impressionism which appears to be one of the most admired types of painting at this period, or he may find an affinity for the Surrealists, the Primitives, the Cubists or the Vorticists. The passing admiration which the pupil may show for particular schools or individuals should not be discouraged. This phase is symptomatic of a growing mind and of a developing awareness of man's struggle for expression in visual form. The main task of the teacher at this period is to provide the learners with a great variety of examples of expression representative of many cultures and schools of thought. Eventually the pupil, supported by a reasonably broad knowledge of his artistic heritage, will usually arrive at a personal mode of expression.

It will be recognized that many pupils in the early part of middle adolescence are not concerned with design and technique in picture-making. The general trend, however, is for design and technique to improve so that at some time during this period one may expect to discover some noteworthy examples of output. Mass and space begin to be considered in more effective relationships so that the backgrounds of paintings tend noticeably to become an integral part of compositions. In addition, the masses become more related by means of a consciously arranged overlapping and exhibit a greater variety of shapes and relative sizes. Recognition of space as an element of design often leads to an achievement of depth or volume in output and is made apparent by means of a more competent handling of colour tones, linear perspective and the placement of masses. Line becomes more sensitive and texture is used in an increasingly significant manner. Technique tends to become more personal while many compositions appear which present a reasonable variety and unity.

The outstanding skills developed during middle adolescence include facility in draughtsmanship, in linear perspective and in the handling of media for specific effects with special reference to using tints and shades of colour, preparing and underpainting surfaces, combining media and the handling of tools and equipment. The development of such skills presupposes efficient teaching.

The habits of work of the middle adolescent are often erratic. Their span of attention may sometimes be very short, while at other times they will work in a concentrated manner for relatively long periods. Their whole attitude to work may vary from inattention and an obvious dislike for picture-making to rapt concentration and delight in this activity.

88   ART EDUCATION DURING ADOLESCENCE

31 "Noon-hour Whistle"—a painting in tempera by an 18-year-old boy. His artistic skills and insights are becoming well developed as a result of expert teaching and an uninterrupted art programme in his school.

(iv) *Later Adolescence (about Grades X, XI, and XII).*

The subjects selected by pupils in later adolescence are reminiscent of those chosen by pupils in the middle period. Gradually the pupils begin to show marked preferences for subject matter and will produce many pictures of varying aspects of the same theme. One pupil might occupy himself largely with social themes, another upon fanciful subject-matter and yet another with architectural features of buildings found in the environment. (See Plate **6**.) Topics are sometimes selected from themes based upon the pupil's plans for the future, or music and literature may form the basis of illustration. Often a subject is chosen not because of its literary content but rather for the interesting pattern produced by the juxtaposition of one object related to others. Thus still-life, life and landscape become of major importance to pupils

PICTURE-MAKING BY ADOLESCENTS 89

in later adolescence. (See Plates **32** and **33**.) Since the range of subject matter selected is almost as wide as that found in professional output, it is difficult to set down a list of representative titles. The following titles were used with success by the pupils studied and they serve to illustrate to some extent the wide scope of subject matter selected during later adolescence:

>Old buildings.
>Back gardens.
>Shipyards.
>Oil tanks.
>Roof tops.
>Interior of a mine.
>Sea shells.
>Marionettes.
>Ballerina.
>Still-life with machinery.
>Character study of an old man.
>Portrait of a young child.
>Self-portrait.
>Labour.
>Sunday in the park.
>The wedding.
>Pickets on Queen Street.
>Crowd at the football game.
>Religious ceremony.
>Valley of the Don River.
>Hillside farm—Eastern Ontario.
>Main Street.
>Scene from *King Lear* (Shakespearean Festival, Stratford).
>*Façade* (Poems set to Music, Sitwell & Lambert).
>Aspiration.
>Four Horsemen of the Apocalypse.

Much of the output during later adolescence includes qualities associated with any successful production in art. A nice fusion of design, technique and subject matter begins to be apparent. The work often is very personal to its author and exhibits a blending of emotional and intellectual statement. If the pupil has been taught effectively, his technique or style of painting becomes more or less distinct. Pupils in later adolescence may alter their style from time to time, but experimentation at this period is not as marked as was previously the case. Now the pupils seem to be consolidating their discoveries, some of which were made in middle adolescence. Skill continues to develop in connection with technique, draughtsmanship and composition. (See Plate 31.) Increasing confidence in his own powers as well as a developing vision assist the pupil in the development of these skills. During later adolescence many pupils will work for long periods with concentrated effort, not only upon new themes and techniques, but also upon those which are familiar to them. They do so apparently to achieve greater perfection—an attitude which is characteristic of the artist.

5. Characteristics of Picture-Making Influenced by the Sex of the Adolescent

The sex as well as the stage of physical, mental, emotional and social maturation of the adolescent may have an effect upon his picture-making. This effect is more apparent in the case of pupils who achieve considerable success in their work than it is in the output of mediocre pupils.

Subject matter is sometimes influenced by the sex of the pupil. Many boys tend to keep aloof from any topic of feminine interest. A few girls, on the other hand, may select subject matter having interest for both sexes. A number of representative topics selected by boys include self-improvement of mind and body; developments in science and industry; adventure; biography; travel; and current events. (See Plate 25.) The topics selected by many girls include romantic meetings; social events; fashion displays; happenings related to clubs and societies; sports where costume is an attraction or where there is a mingling of sexes. (See Plate 24.)

When differences in the viewpoint of expression are apparent, boys tend to be more logical than girls. Boys are frequently more concerned with the functional qualities of depicted objects. Replacing an element of humour often seen in the work of boys is one of sentiment in girls' work. It is not unusual to find as far as middle adolescence both these elements being carried beyond a state of subtlety.

PICTURE-MAKING BY ADOLESCENTS

32 "Milkweed"—a painting in tempera. This original and competent abstract work is based upon observation of a plant found in the local environment. A spray gun was used in parts of the background. The 19-year-old painter has ability in art which is being encouraged by commendable teaching practices.

When differences of technique may be noted, the work of boys is frequently bolder and stronger than that of girls although the characteristic vigour of the work produced during early adolescence may show marked refinement as boys mature. The work of girls may often be recognized by a greater delicacy, sensitivity and sometimes fussiness. Boys tend to work more quickly than girls; often brief and blunt in their statement, they tend to omit detail which girls may include in their paintings.

The obvious differences in picture-making between boys and girls mentioned above will perhaps have no great significance for the liberal teacher who employs teaching methods which allow for individual differences. Of greater importance to him perhaps is the matter of fluctuations in the standard of work produced by boys and girls. Marked fluctuations of this nature occur during adolescence in the art output of both sexes, although they become less pronounced during later adolescence. The fluctuations in standard are more noticeable with girls. In many cases the standard of their work seems to be influenced during menstruation. At such periods standards tend to deteriorate and the element which seems to be most affected in this respect is that of colour.

The fact that fluctuations occur, in boys at irregular intervals and in girls at more regular intervals, leads one not to expect of young people any uniform progress in their art production. It may be pointed out in this connection that because these fluctuations in ability occur, any appraisal of pupils based upon art examinations cannot be reliable.

6. Picture-Making by Gifted Adolescents

During childhood the gifted learner does not present notable problems for the sympathetic teacher of art. Such a child will pass through the various stages of pictorial expression with greater rapidity than will his normal classmates. An enriched programme in art to meet his needs and to keep pace with his rate of learning is generally all the special educational treatment he requires.

During adolescence the problem of the gifted individual becomes more acute. In order to gain greater insight into the problems related to gifted adolescents the Ontario Department of Education has for several years sponsored special classes in art for about 50 of these people each year in which they might be carefully and systematically studied. These gifted pupils were selected from an urban and suburban area having a total population of nearly one and a half million.

Difficulty was experienced in selecting those pupils who were truly gifted in art. Some of the pupils who appeared to have talent were in reality clever with their hands, but lacked the vision necessary to produce artistic forms. Some on the other hand, while displaying real talent, lacked certain personal qualities including initiative, drive and the ability to see work through to its logical conclusion. A select group could, however, be recognized as specially gifted and at the same time capable of making full use of their talents.

How does one recognize a gifted pupil? One may say that "gifted is as gifted does." The pupil who consistently produces a relatively large amount of sensitive and original art work of a standard higher than that found in the output of his fellows may be suspected of being gifted. Such pupils it was found occur rarely, and they almost invariably achieve high scores in I.Q. tests in spite of the fact that such tests do not measure special aptitudes. It was found that most of the gifted pupils studied seemed to be well-adjusted emotionally and socially although they came from varying social, ethnic and economic groups. Because of their intense interest in their work they caused no disciplinary problems, but instead were quietly co-operative with their teachers and their classmates. Most of these pupils, moreover, had a well-developed sense of humour.

The group of gifted pupils exhibited as a class certain peculiarities. The boys frequently produced work of higher merit than the girls, but the girls produced meritorious work more consistently. Most of the pupils became discouraged from time to time and then required guidance, but the boys tended to become discouraged more often than did the girls. All these pupils nevertheless welcomed honest criticism even if it was at times severe. All of them were most critical of their own output and the majority of their self-criticisms although tending to be too harsh were penetrating. In design

33 "Still-life Painting in Oils," the work of a talented 18-year-old boy who has been fortunate enough to receive expert guidance in art.

work these pupils welcomed specific problems related to the various elements. They did not appear to like group work as much as they did working individually.

It is self-evident that the teacher of gifted pupils must, himself, be especially talented both as a teacher and as a producer of art forms. In the classes under discussion it was found expedient and effective to invite specialists to speak to the groups, to display their work and to give demonstrations in those fields of art which were not within the competence of the regular staff. The gifted pupil requires teachers with special aptitudes in the art work under their consideration.

The teaching techniques including motivation and guidance which must be employed in an art programme for normal pupils were found to be also necessary and effective for gifted individuals. Gifted pupils require the stimulation of new materials and of many varied experiences in life to be used for expressive purposes. They also require timely and effective guidance. The task of the teacher of the gifted in the matter of stimulation is not so great, however, as it is for the teacher of normal pupils. Gifted pupils are quick to establish goals for expression and to find meanings, visual relationships and points of view in their environment. Although the teacher has fewer personal demands from his gifted pupils with regard to motivation, he has far greater demands made upon him for guidance. Gifted pupils continually seek guidance since they enjoy an ability to isolate and to define problems as they arise in their work. It might be mentioned here that the gifted pupils demand the greatest honesty and sincerity, both in guidance and in appraisal of their own work.

Because the gifted adolescent may profit from teaching at a pace beyond the normal, and because also he requires expert guidance at relatively frequent intervals, it is obvious that he should be given special opportunities in art education. If these opportunities cannot be offered during the regular school day, they should be provided in after-school or in week-end classes. Extra classes outside the regular school programme appear to offer a more suitable solution to the problem of teaching the gifted. The superior pupil may attend such extra classes without incurring charges of being different or snobbish which are likely to arise if he is isolated from his fellows in regular school classes. There is also the advantage in these classes of being able to recruit for short periods certain specialists in various art fields.

It may be assumed that every community of any size has among its numbers some adolescents especially clever in art and it is greatly to be hoped that their rare gifts may not be neglected.

7. Summary

Picture-making appears to be the most flexible activity in art by which an adolescent may express his thoughts, feelings and attitudes. A deterioration in the normal standard of output in this field results if the programme is interrupted. Substitute studies in art cannot compensate for the abilities acquired by means of picture-making. Secondary education should give greater emphasis to art, particularly in the higher grades.

Adolescents exhibit a more or less regular pattern of success in producing pictures which, if other things are equal, is governed by the general developmental stages in which the pupils find themselves. The sex of the learner has some bearing upon picture-making. Both sexes exhibit fluctuations in their output, with changes occurring irregularly with boys and more regularly with girls. Since these fluctuations occur, the results derived from examinations in art tend to be unreliable.

Gifted pupils require special educational treatment in order to profit as fully as possible from their talents.

ADDITIONAL READING:

Viktor Lowenfeld. *Creative and Mental Growth.* (Revised) New York: The Macmillan Company, 1952.

Kimon Nicolaïdes. *The Natural Way to Draw.* Boston: Houghton-Mifflin Company, 1941.

Ralph M. Pearson. *The New Art Education.* New York: Harper and Brothers, 1941.

Chapter VII

A PROGRAMME OF OPTIONAL ART ACTIVITIES FOR ADOLESCENTS

1. Research into Optional Activities

Research concerned with optional activities in art was conducted in 44 classrooms suitably staffed and equipped for different types of work. Wherever it appeared practical to do so, pupils at all levels of development enrolled in grades seven to twelve participated in this work. Careful notes were made of the varying degrees of success which pupils of different ages might be expected to find in each activity. The question of how many activities each pupil should elect was considered. Attention was also given to the competence in each field which a teacher should enjoy in order to teach adolescents. A study was made of the type of guidance which these pupils should receive so that the activities would be educationally effective. The most practical methods by which the pupils might develop designs in connection with some of the work were also considered. Finally the extent to which the pupils might profit from group activities in art was studied. This chapter offers comments about these topics in the light of the observations made while the optional activities were in progress in Ontario classrooms.

2. Some Factors Affecting the Choice of Optional Activities

It is almost impossible to envisage an art programme for adolescents which fails to include both picture-making and a consideration of some related historical developments. Picture-making is the most flexible art form by which the majority of young people may express themselves artistically. A study of historical trends in art is prerequisite for an understanding of man's struggle to master his environment and to improve upon his conditions of life. Pupils who fail to enjoy experiences in these two branches of art would be deficient, indeed, in their general education. Many other activities on the other hand may be considered as optional studies. These activities broaden an art programme and add interest to it, and in doing so they are important additions to the study of art. From them the teacher and the class may select those which may meet the needs and satisfy the interests of the pupils. The number of different options which should engage the attention of any pupil cannot be stated because each person works at a different rate of speed from his fellows and because some activities require more time to be spent on them than others. It may be observed, however, that more mature pupils usually wish to work in fewer areas than the less mature since the former develop a greater number of problems, master more skills related to tools and materials, and acquire deeper insights as their work progresses.

As suggested in the third chapter of this book, the competence of the teacher is one of the important factors regulating the selection of optional studies. Whereas the art teacher of young children may offer an almost endless list of materials with which to work and may provide sufficient guidance to help the children achieve satisfactory results, such is not the case with the teacher of adolescents. At this level the critical faculties of the pupils are sharp and little short of mastery of materials, tools and techniques will satisfy them. The teacher will find that the curve of development in ability and success described for picture-making in the previous chapter will be approximated in any other art activities performed by adolescents. While the early adolescent will find difficulty in his work and will exhibit fluctuating degrees of interest in it, and application to it, the more mature pupils will if given adequate guidance, develop not only praiseworthy attitudes and strong personal interests, but also remarkable skills. (See Plates **34**, **35** and **37**.) The teacher must himself be expert in any activity he sponsors for his more mature pupils.

The conditions determining the choice of optional activities, as well as including the interests and needs of the pupils and the competence of the teacher, will also include the materials, tools and general accommodation and equipment available. Some activities require very little extra equipment and accommodation beyond those needed for picture-making. Other activities call for specialized items in order that the work may be reasonably included in the art programme.

A PROGRAMME OF OPTIONAL ART ACTIVITIES 99

34 Non-objective sculpture in wood. In producing this work the young sculptor has gained valuable experience in three-dimensional design.

3. Guidance of Pupils Working at Optional Activities

The list of activities to be discussed in this chapter is not intended to be too exhaustive, nor are the remarks about them planned to be specific. Each of the activities mentioned requires a detailed study beyond the scope of this volume. Some excellent publications are available on most of the topics listed and are mentioned at the end of the chapter. The teacher cannot for the most part master the activities outside a studio under the control of an expert. Only in such a setting can a teacher of adolescents acquire the necessary skills and insights to permit him to offer instruction in the fields of art described. The following discussion includes merely a list of what are considered to be some basic activities within the scope

35 Paper sculpture involving a measured line. This disciplined work has resulted in architectural types of design.

of art education. If these activities are to be beneficial to the pupils from the standpoint of general education, much will depend upon the forms of guidance offered by the teacher. Each of the activities may be taught creatively or dictatorially. If they are taught creatively they will assist the pupils to develop personally toward the maturity they seek. If taught dictatorially they will allow the pupils to gain only narrow skills.

In many of the activities, three-dimensional materials will be employed. By means of these materials taste can be developed, or it can just as easily be degraded. Fine materials can be used in either a worthy manner, or an unworthy one. As a result of improper guidance students may learn to debase the qualities of wood, metal or plastic just as readily as they may be encouraged to treat materials with disciplined precision, style and taste.

4. Developing Original Patterns and Designs

A number of activities to be mentioned, such as linoleum-block printing, leave room for the development of surface patterns. In this work guidance becomes extremely important. A pattern should be developed creatively. If its source lies in the objective world then the natural object must be "worked over" and brought to the degree of abstraction desired by the designer in terms of the relationship he sees for it between the material in use and the type of decoration which would best bring out the qualities of the material. Manifestly, only those aspects of the objective world which are familiar to a designer and for which he has some feeling, may be used in the pattern being created. Inspiration may come from items as diverse as local flowers and trees, the flight of birds, the marks made by wheels in the snow, rows of rooftops with their television antennae, children at play, or the skyline of a city. If the designer is not familiar with sailing yachts he will not use them in his design. If he has never visited Mexico he will not draw Mexicans sleeping under cactus plants. Only observations from known and felt experiences can be utilized if the resulting pattern is to ring true.

Apart from the objective world, there exists only one other legitimate source of inspiration for the development of design or pattern. This may be found in the play of the elements of design manipulated without reference to objective experience. The resulting patterns are called "non-objective" and may be a striking, though usually less personal art form. As in the act of creating abstract forms the designer of non-objective patterns must consider his work as an entirely personal and creative endeavour. (See Plate **36**.)

In some of the classes observed, the teachers failed to emphasize originality, and as a result the pupils produced badly designed objects. When pupils "borrow" designs and "apply" them to whatever they are making, invariably an aesthetic chaos is to be seen. Only in those classrooms where design was created from experience was the output commendable.

Although the designs produced by young people, whether abstract or non-objective, are expected to be original, the pupils should have an opportunity of studying the best examples of professional output in any field under consideration. That the pupils will be influenced by the work studied is not to be denied. Any creating person goes about with his eyes open and he finds from time to time that he has modified his output because of his observation. Some of the most highly regarded artists have been influenced by the output of others; Modigliani, for example, shows the influences of African sculpture; Matisse, that of Oriental art and of Persian art forms in particular. Yet the work of these painters and of many others one might mention remains as personal and creative as any to be seen. These qualities are exhibited because the artists, while being moved by the work of others, have persisted in making all relevant experience their own. It is partly because of their contact with the powerful productions of others that they gain insight into the meaning of art and that their own work becomes richer and even more personal.

5. Optional Activities for Individual Work

The following activities have been selected for special mention because they appeared to allow adolescents the greatest scope for individual initiative and expression. All the activities, with the exception of one or two noted in this section, proved to be suitable for pupils enrolled in every grade from seven to twelve. Some simplified methods must often be used with the younger pupils, but it was obvious that teachers who were familiar with this work had no difficulty in accommodating any particular activity to the abilities of pupils at different levels of development.

(i) *Pattern-Making on Textiles.*

Patterns may be applied to textiles by means of a number of well-known techniques. Among these are included linoleum-block printing and stencilling which may be used by pupils in all grades, and silk-screen printing, which may be taught most effectively from grade nine to grade twelve. Some teachers insist that, rather than drawing and painting patterns in advance of the technical operations involved, the pupils should experiment directly with the tools and materials to be used. Later when insight into the technique has been gained, the

A PROGRAMME OF OPTIONAL ART ACTIVITIES 103

36 Linoleum block-printing on textile. The pupil has experimented directly both in carving linoleum and in printing on the textile so that he might gain a greater knowledge of the materials and techniques involved.

pupils may then draw and paint more carefully designed patterns before printing begins. It is maintained that only after direct preliminary experimentation with materials and tools can designs be made intelligently in relation to the media employed. (See Plate 36.)

The patterns developed for textiles frequently take the form of "all-over" designs in which a unit is repeated according to arrangements known as "alternating", "half-drop" and "full-drop". To require pupils to cover a large sheet of paper by carefully drawing and painting the unit many times over may often be wasteful of time and energy. Unless the pupil wishes to complete a sheet of repeated units, it seems reasonable to suggest that he be required to draw and paint only the number of units necessary to allow him to visualize the effects desired.

The printing methods mentioned above may also be employed on paper. They are particularly valuable in the production of programme covers, place cards and posters in which large numbers of a similar design are required.

(ii) *Loom Weaving.*

This activity requires both equipment and materials which are relatively expensive and which necessitate a large area of floor and storage space. Although loom weaving comes within the scope of art education, a satisfactory arrangement may often be made by which this activity is taught in the home economics department where even advanced weaving with four-harness looms is often studied.

Although the mechanics of operating a loom are exacting and the movements involved repetitious, much of the designing, particularly with regard to the elements of texture and colour can be most creative. The film *Homespun* (Museum of Modern Art, New York), in which the weaver performs all the operations from shearing the wool and making her own dyes to weaving the most delicate and original designs, is worthy of particular attention.

Loom weaving seems to afford the greatest satisfactions for those who practice it and not infrequently it becomes an absorbing leisure-time occupation. Pupils in all grades may be successful in this work.

(iii) *Sculpture.*

Sculpture is an excellent activity to increase the learner's sensitivity in the manipulation of volumes in space. Often following a study of sculpture an added strength is found in a pupil's drawing and painting as a result of the insight gained into three-dimensional forms. Certain materials such as stone, metal and wood are greatly favoured by physically developing youth, for they may pit their strength and energies against a resisting substance.

37 Objective paper sculpture. The design is highly stylized, but is based upon objective experience.

Suitable materials for sculpture by more mature pupils include plastics and stone. (See Plate **23**.) Materials for sculpture by younger pupils include cardboard, paper and wood, although older pupils, as well, will find a challenge in these materials. (See Plates **34** and **35**.) A branch of sculpture which includes not only the usual three dimensions, but also what might be considered a fourth consisting of a relationship between masses and spaces in movement, is to be found in the making of "mobiles". (See Plate **14**.) This is a delicate art form lending itself to the use of all manner of materials and offering unlimited possibilities for creative thinking. Although mobile sculpture leans heavily towards non-objective forms, its inspiration may be derived from movements in nature as one may observe in the poetic film: *Works of Calder* (Museum of Modern Art, New York). Mobile sculpture is suitable for pupils in all grades.

(iv) *Lettering and Poster-making.*

Lettering and poster-making at the professional level demand highly developed technical skills of a specific and somewhat limited nature. Because of this, one may hesitate to introduce these activities into a programme of general art education for adolescents. Badly designed letters and posters are to be condemned so that if these forms are to be produced at all, they must be done so effectively.

One method to circumnavigate the long and relatively restrictive drills associated with the drawing and painting of letters and posters is to use a montage technique. By means of this technique, poster-making, if not lettering, may be kept at a creative level until the work is complete. The alphabet employed for the headings may be a sans-serif style of constant thicknesses. In this way the difficulties and intricacies of the serifs and of the varying width of the Roman letters may be avoided. Although the Roman alphabet is graceful and legible and might be studied incidentally, it presents difficulties of reproduction which almost forbid its use in a class outside of a technical school. In the matter of sub-headings, the pupils might be encouraged to use a legible script based upon their own handwriting. This might readily be rendered with lettering pens. Having cut the letters for the headings out of paper and produced the script on various other pieces of paper for the sub-headings, the pupils will then be ready to make final arrangements upon a support of cardboard or paper of suitable colour. When the final composition is considered to be satisfactory the items of the montage may be fixed in place. Additional decoration with spray guns, or a montage of confetti, for example, may be added to tie the composition together.

It is recommended that unless pupils especially desire formal exercises in lettering and poster-making in order to perfect their skills in these forms, the teacher should attempt to eliminate such drills and substitute easier techniques. One might add that in a general art programme, it is preferable to produce posters only when a real need for them arises in the school. Then, like all the other art produced they should be creative. The montage method is suitable for pupils in all grades.

(v) *Work in Ceramics.*

This ancient craft calls for much special equipment and either a room or a portion of the art room devoted to nothing but ceramics. (See Plate 2.) In company with weaving, a study of ceramics brings the greatest satisfactions to the producer and the craft frequently becomes a leisure-time activity. Like sculpture, it is particularly valuable in teaching the pupil to respect material and to appreciate functional and basic design. (See Plate 13.) More mature students may learn not only the techniques associated with the coil method together with the production of "free forms", but also those of the potter's wheel. Pupils in all grades can learn the techniques of firing and glazing as well as those associated with the manipulation of clay.

(vi) *Metal Work and Enamelling.*

The courses offered in industrial art shops for boys usually devote considerable attention to the production of art forms in metal. Many girls also are attracted to metal work particularly in connection with jewellery making, so that special arrangements might profitably be made for them to use the metal-working shops in schools where the art room is not equipped for this work. Closely associated with work in metal is the ancient craft of enamelling. This is becoming more popular in secondary schools where some remarkably interesting output is to be seen. Charming results may be achieved relatively quickly once the techniques have been mastered. Where only simple snipping, filing and hammering are required, pupils in all grades may work in metal. Those techniques such as enamelling, which require intense heat, should be reserved at least until pupils reach middle adolescence.

(vii) *Photographic Techniques.*

Another activity which is gaining quickly in popularity is that associated with photographic techniques employed for the production of design. The art form known as the "photogram" and the technique called "photomontage" may be used both to produce the most original and striking patterns and to help pupils gain further insight into the elements of light and shade. Since cameras are not required, the equipment is relatively inexpensive. Pupils in all grades may be successful in this work.

(viii) *Leather work.*

Surveys have indicated that the most popular material with adult groups engaged in crafts is leather and its popularity is also high with young people. Unfortunately although leather is a fine material in itself, it is often abused in the type of pattern which has been applied to it. Leather work can and should be creative. The basic design of any object should be planned by its maker, while any pattern tooled upon its surface should be original and in good taste. The tools and equipment required for work in leather are relatively inexpensive although the leather itself is usually costly. Leather work has the advantage in the art room of being clean and for the most part quiet, and is eminently suitable for pupils at all levels.

(ix) *Etching Processes and "Resist Techniques".*

Although they are more the province of the technical than the general school, a number of interesting but exacting processes known generally as etching may be taught to senior pupils. Most of these processes call for highly technical knowledge on the part of the teacher and some special equipment. They include etching with acids on a zinc or copper plate, dry point etching, lithography, soft ground etching and work in the mezzotint, aquatint, and monotype methods.

A process related to those mentioned above is scratchboard work. Pupils at any level may find success with this material since it involves simply cutting through a dark surface of a specially prepared board to a light background. Problems associated with line, light and shade are accentuated by means of this process.

What are known as "resist techniques" add greatly to the pupils' interest in graphic work. These techniques are based upon the practice of shedding liquids from selected areas of a drawing or painting where a substance for the purpose has been placed. Such substances as rubber cement or wax serve admirably in this kind of work. The ordinary wax-crayons used in elementary schools may be employed to add colour to "resist" areas. Repeated ink or water-colour washes over sections of a drawing on which "resist" areas have been carefully arranged bring interesting effects. (See Plate **38**.) A mixture of such media as water-colour, india ink, tempera paint and conté crayon may be effectively employed in this work.

6. Optional Group Activities

One of the most important aims of general education is the development of the individual within his social group and art, being part of education, must contribute to the achievement of this aim. Although most of the work in art must be produced by individuals working by themselves, there is also a group life in the art class to be fostered by means of a number of art activities. That pupils should participate in group work from time to time as the occasions present themselves is greatly to be desired.

Only those activities which could not be successfully completed by an individual working independently can be classed as group work. Adolescents, with some exceptions in the case of the gifted pupil, will readily take part in a well-chosen project involving the participation of several people. Among the most interesting and challenging group activities are the following: mural making; marionette work and puppetry; stage craft; and model building. Pupils at any level may participate in all these activities.

(i) *Mural Making*.

Murals made by adolescents should be more than just enlarged pictures. The making of a mural is a specialized activity which brings with it a number of problems arising from the size of the work, the unique type of design required so that the solid quality of the wall is respected, the materials to be employed and the subject matter to be selected. The history of mural making is inspiring and should be mentioned while this activity is engaging the attention of the class. The heroic

38 "Wilson's Snipe"—a work in water-colour and ink by a gifted student. A "resist technique" has been used involving rubber cement.

efforts of Michelangelo and his monumental murals in the Sistine Chapel constitute one of the most moving passages in the story of man's artistic endeavour. The experiments of Diego Rivera by which his murals have evolved as strong, vigorous and yet simple expressions upon a noble scale deserve the attention of young people. Many schools would become more attractive by means of a well-placed mural. The subjects chosen for a mural produced by the pupils should, of course, be based upon their own experience and interests.

(ii) *Marionette Work, Puppetry and Stagecraft.*

Marionette work and puppetry include much more than the making of the little figures. Puppets and marionettes should be produced with the idea of staging a production of some kind. The studies related to this field include costume-designing, building a puppet stage, arrangement of lighting, *décor*, stage management, manipulation of the characters and often the selection of suitable music. The possibilities for strong correlation with the study of both spoken and written English are obvious. The same opportunities to write and present original plays and music which are available in stagecraft in general, are to be found in puppetry and marionette work.

Because of the large amount of designing and broad creative endeavour demanded in any form of stagecraft, this field may rightly come within the scope of art education.

(iii) *Model Building.*

The co-operative planning and producing of model communities in miniature is an activity of great importance to adolescents. It must be observed that most communities in existence today would be improved had timely thought been given to their planning. We are finding to our discomfort that the lack of planning in our cities and towns has led in many instances to a condition approaching solidified chaos which will cost untold millions of dollars to correct. Perhaps if a larger proportion of the general population were to gain a greater insight into the problems of reconstruction which face us, we might make more rapid progress in their solution. It is conceivable also, in spite of economic problems which always beset community planning, that with a wider and more informed interest in the topic we might avoid many mistakes in the future.

It will be seen that the group activity of planning communities in miniature has practical as well as aesthetic merit. The activity may readily be correlated with that fascinating part of history concerned with community planning and depicted with great insight by Mumford in *The Culture of Cities.*

(iv) *Display Techniques.*

A group activity of some importance mentioned in another connection in Chapter II, is that of planning and posting displays of art work in the school. Display techniques demand a number of specific abilities related to space arrangements, the establishing of centres of interest and the creation of design in depth which may be acquired only after careful study.

39 Manipulating marionettes in preparation for a show. These young adolescents are enjoying participation in a group activity.

7. Summary

A programme of art for adolescents, while providing opportunities for study in the fields of picture-making and history, should offer in addition several optional activities. The options to be provided will depend upon the needs and interests of the pupils, the competence of the teacher in the various fields, as well as the materials, tools and general accommodation and equipment available. The guidance offered by the teacher, whether in relation to two- or three-dimensional materials, must encourage the production of original designs. Any patterns or designs which the pupils develop in connection with these materials should be derived only from personal experience. Such experience comes either from the objective world or from the manipulation of the elements of design to produce non-objective forms.

Optional studies include both individual and group activities. It is highly recommended that adolescents participate occasionally in art activities in which a group is involved.

ADDITIONAL READING:

Raymond A. Ballinger. *Lettering Art in Modern Use.* New York: Rheinhold Publishing Co., 1952.

Marjorie Batchelder. *The Puppet Theatre Handbook.* New York and London: Harper and Brothers, 1947.

Kenneth F. Bates. *Enamelling, Principles and Practice.* Cleveland and New York: The World Publishing Company, 1951.

Harriet J. Brown. *Hand Weaving for Pleasure and Profit.* New York: Harper and Brothers, 1952.

Julia Hamlin Duncan. *How to Make Pottery and Ceramic Sculpture—20 Graded Projects.* New York: Simon and Schuster and Museum of Modern Art, 1947.

Hans Feibusch. *Mural Painting.* London: Adam and Charles Black, 1946.

Ruth Green Harris and Gerolami Piccole. *Techniques of Sculpture.* New York: Harper and Brothers, 1942.

C. G. Holme. *Lettering of Today.* London: Adam and Charles Black, 1946.

Mary Grace Johnston. *Paper Sculpture.* Worcester, Mass: The Davis Press, Inc., 1952.

John Lynch. *How to Make Mobiles.* New York: Studio Publications Inc., in association with Thomas Y. Crowell Co., 1953.

Charles J. Mortin and Victor D'Amico. *How to Make Modern Jewelry.* New York: Museum of Modern Art and Simon and Schuster, (Distributors), 1949.

Lewis Mumford. *The Culture of Cities.* New York: Harcourt Brace and Company, Inc., 1938.

Peter Noble. *British Theatre.* London: British Yearbooks, 1946.

Jacques Schnier. *Sculpture in Modern America.* Berkeley and Los Angeles: University of California Press, 1948.

James Johnson Sweeney. *Henry Moore.* New York: Museum of Modern Art, 1947.

D. Kenneth Winebrenner. *Jewelry Making as an Art Expression.* Worcester, Mass.: The Davis Press, Inc., 1952.

CONCLUSION

THE NATURE OF ADOLESCENCE AS A PERIOD OF PHYSICAL, intellectual, emotional and social growth has been discussed in the preceding chapters of this book. No one can study this phase of life without being struck both by the great potentialities inherent in each young person who enters this period, and by the enormous influence which a teacher can exert at this time. Sensing goals which must be reached if he is to arrive at a normal and balanced maturity, the pupil is receptive to educational practices which he considers to be of value to him in meeting his present needs and in attaining his goals.

Art lends itself readily to a form of education which is both acceptable and beneficial to adolescents. With its subject matter arising from the pupil's experience, and with its flexibility as to the modes of expression which may be employed, art may be used to suit most of the varying types of personality to be found among young people. Because adolescents may develop profound interests and find deep satisfactions in art activities, the intellectual and emotional disciplines inherent in these pursuits may work their beneficial effects upon all those pupils whose energies they absorb. Art demands of the creating person the greatest honesty and the highest sense of values, so that in time the student who submerges himself in this work may begin to develop a personal philosophy of worthy conduct and belief having application to any field of human endeavour.

The education of an individual is not complete unless he has learned to participate to the full extent of his abilities in affairs involving a group. As well as exerting beneficial effects upon the individual pupil, art may assist him to develop insights into the techniques of working with others. Many art activities allow the young person naturally and creatively to solve numerous problems which arise when people gather together for the purpose of thinking as a group.

The energies of young people, which are always seeking some outlet can travel in any direction, either good or bad. The vandalism of gangs of youth mentioned from time to time in the daily newspapers, are a manifestation of the fact that young people seek expression, and that their energies have not been guided along creative lines. The creative person is not a destroyer. That all adolescents should be directed towards creative endeavours is obviously most necessary. In art may be found a channel of major importance in which youth may find a positive, constructive, and entirely worthy form of expression.

Art education during adolescence calls for a carefully chosen pedagogy. If the teaching methods used are influenced by the great tradition of man's artistic heritage, they will tend to be effective. Throughout the ages, man in his attempt to express his feelings either of wonder and delight at the world in which he finds himself, or his approval or disapproval of the actions of other men with whom he comes in contact, has painstakingly developed ways of working, thinking and feeling which are characteristic of all those who produce art forms. These practices which have evolved are founded upon the tradition that the creating person must have control of the tools and media, together with the ideas and feelings associated with expressive acts. For the teacher of adolescents to deny the necessary freedoms of thought and action which are traditional to artistic endeavour is to prevent the pupils from participating in art. In allowing these freedoms, the teacher in no way removes disciplinary measures. One cannot be responsible for artistic acts without exerting a high degree of self-discipline. The tasks of sifting experiences and of resolving these experiences into design forms call for the greatest personal disciplines on the part of those pupils who enter into them.

To allow these freedoms in no way eliminates the need of guidance in the art class. Whatever guidance is given must be timely and closely associated with the pupils' problems as they arise during the course of expression and must be supported by exceptional professional insight into both education and art.

For a young person to derive full benefit from his studies in art, he must continue this work throughout the entire period of adolescence. No field of study can duplicate entirely what art has to offer. The kind of thinking in relation to experiences, tools and materials found in art is unique to this field. Those young people who terminate their artistic studies in early adolescence, a stage of human development full of personal difficulties, can never realize their full potentialities in this work. Only by continuing a programme of art education throughout their whole school life, can they discover their own artistic powers and gain insights into the true nature of art.

In art may be found a field of study which, if educational conditions are right, may contribute in a unique fashion to the development of youth. Elementary schools have made enormous strides in bringing art into the service of general education. Many of those responsible for educational matters are now realizing that this subject may be equally, if not more, beneficial in secondary education than it is at the elementary level, so that we may look forward confidently to an increased use of art education in the secondary schools of our educational structure.